The Life *of* Jesus Christ

A BIOGRAPHICAL OVERVIEW
of the LIFE *of* CHRIST

JAMES STALKER

ANEKO
PRESS

We love hearing from our readers. Please contact us
at www.anekopress.com/questions-comments with
any questions, comments, or suggestions.

Aneko Press

www.anekopress.com
Aneko Press, Life Sentence Publishing, and our logos are trademarks of
Life Sentence Publishing, Inc.
203 E. Birch Street
P.O. Box 652
Abbotsford, WI 54405
BIOGRAPHY & AUTOBIOGRAPHY / Religious
Paperback ISBN: 978-1-62245-735-9
eBook ISBN: 978-1-62245-736-6
10 9 8 7 6 5 4 3 2
Available where books are sold

Contents

Preface

(Adapted from the Preface to the Twenty-ninth Edition)

The demand for *The Life of Jesus Christ* by James Stalker continues with amazing regularity. Year after year, edition has followed edition since the book was first published nearly a hundred and fifty years ago. It is known in every English-speaking country and has been translated into many foreign languages.

We now find it necessary to reprint this noteworthy book again. The reasons for its continued success are not difficult to find. The details of the life of Christ flow together here in the reader's mind and shape themselves into an easily understood whole.

Only someone thoroughly equipped in point of scholarship, skillful in condensing, and completely attuned to his subject could have prepared such a clear, concise, and understandable narrative of the earthly life of the Son of God. Fascinating to read and contemplate, it is also invaluable as a textbook in revealing the manners and customs of Jesus' day.

Chapter 1

The Birth, Infancy, and Youth of Jesus

The Nativity

Augustus was sitting on the throne of the Roman Empire, and the touch of his finger could set the machinery of government in motion over just about the entire civilized world. He was proud of his power and wealth, and it was one of his favorite activities to compile a register of the populations and revenues of his vast dominions.

So he issued an edict, as the evangelist Luke says, *that all the world should be taxed* (Luke 2:1). More accurately, the words probably mean that a census that would serve as a basis for future taxation would be taken of all his subjects. One of the countries affected by this decree was Israel, whose king, Herod the Great, was a vassal of Augustus. It set the whole land in motion, for in accordance with ancient Jewish custom, the census was not taken at the places where the inhabitants were then residing, but at the places to which they belonged as members of the original twelve tribes.

Among those whom the edict of Augustus forced to travel were a humble pair in the Galilean village of Nazareth: Joseph, the carpenter of the village, and Mary, his espoused wife. They had to travel nearly a hundred miles in order to record themselves in the proper register, for although they were peasants, they had the blood of kings in their veins. They belonged to the ancient and royal town of Bethlehem, in the far south of the country.

Day by day the emperor's will, like an invisible hand, forced them southward along the weary road, until at last, they climbed the rocky ascent that led to the gate of the town. They reached an inn, but found it crowded with strangers who, occupied with the same errand as themselves, had arrived before them. No friendly house opened its door to receive them, and they were eager to make arrangements for their lodging. So, in a corner of the yard of the inn that was also occupied by the beasts of the many travelers, Mary brought forth her firstborn Son that very night. Because there was no other woman's hand to assist her nor a bed to hold Him, she wrapped Him in swaddling clothes and laid Him in a manger (Luke 2:7-12).

This was the manner of the birth of Jesus.[1] I never felt the full emotion of the scene until one day when I was standing in a room of an old inn in the market town of Eisleben, in central Germany. I was told that on that very spot, four centuries earlier, amid the noise of a market day and the bustle of a tavern, the wife of the poor miner, Hans Luther, who happened to be there on business, being surprised like Mary with sudden distress, brought forth in sorrow and poverty the child who was to become Martin Luther, the hero of the Reformation and the maker of modern Europe.

The next morning in Bethlehem, the noise and bustle broke out again in the inn and the yard. The citizens went about their

---

1   The exact date of the birth of Jesus was probably 4 B.C. Luke's statement that the census took place *when Cyrenius was governor of Syria* used to be viewed as a mistake since Cyrenius was governor ten years later. Then the discovery that Cyrenius was governor twice provided a remarkable instance of how alleged mistakes in the Gospels are often made to disappear by further inquiry.

work. The registration proceeded. In the meantime, the greatest event in the history of the world had taken place.

We never know where a great beginning might be happening. Every arrival of a new soul in the world is a mystery and a closed box of possibilities. Only Joseph and Mary knew the tremendous secret – that on her, the peasant maiden and carpenter's bride, had been bestowed the honor of being the mother of Him who was the Messiah of her race, the Savior of the world, and the Son of God.

It had been foretold in ancient prophecy that He would be born on this very spot: *But thou, Bethlehem Ephratah, though thou be little among the thousands of Judah, yet out of thee shall He come forth unto me that is to be ruler in Israel* (Micah 5:2). The proud emperor's decree drove the anxious couple southward, but another hand was leading them on. They were being guided by the hand of Him who, for the accomplishment of His purposes, overrules the plans of emperors and kings, of statesmen and parliaments, even though they might not realize it. Mary and Joseph were being led by the hand of the One who hardened the heart of Pharaoh, called Cyrus like a slave to His foot, and made the mighty Nebuchadnezzar His servant. In the same way, God would overrule the pride and ambition of Augustus for His own far-reaching purpose.

The Group around the Infant

Although Jesus made His entry on the stage of life so humbly and silently; although the citizens of Bethlehem did not dream of what had happened in their midst; although the emperor of Rome did not know that his decree had influenced the birth of a king who was yet to bear rule, not only over the Roman world, but over many lands where Rome's eagles never flew; although the history of mankind went thundering forward the next morning in the channels of its ordinary routine, quite unconscious of the event that had happened – yet it did not completely escape notice.

As the babe leaped in the womb of the aged Elizabeth when the mother of her Lord approached her (Luke 1:41, 44), so when He who brought the new world with Him appeared, there sprang up anticipations and foreshadowings of the truth in various representatives of the old world that was passing away. Through sensitive and waiting souls here and there, there went a dim and half-conscious thrill that drew them around the Infant's cradle. Look at the group that gathered to gaze on Him! It represented in miniature the whole of His future history.

First came the shepherds from the neighboring fields (Luke 2:8-20). That which was unnoticed by the kings and great ones of this world was such a captivating theme to the princes of heaven that they burst the cloak of the invisibility in which they cover themselves in order to express their joy and explain the significance of the great event. Seeking the most worthy hearts to whom they might communicate it, they found them in these simple shepherds who were living the life of contemplation and prayer in the expressive fields where Jacob had kept his flocks, where Boaz and Ruth had been married, and where David, the great Old Testament type, had spent his youth.

It was in these fields that the shepherds, by the study of the secrets and needs of their own hearts, learned far more of the nature of the Savior who was to come than the Pharisee amid the religious pomp of the temple or the scribe burrowing without the seeing eye among the prophecies of the Old Testament. The angel directed them to where the Savior was, and they hurried to the town to find Him. They were the representatives of the peasant people, with honest and good hearts, who later formed the bulk of His disciples.

Next to them came Simeon and Anna (Luke 2:25-38), the representatives of the devout and intelligent students of the Scriptures, who at that time were expecting the appearance of the Messiah and afterward contributed some of His most faithful followers. On the eighth day after His birth, the Child was circumcised (Luke 2:21-24), thus being *made under the law* (Galatians 4:4), entering into the covenant, and inscribing His name in His own blood in the roll of the nation.

Soon thereafter, when the days of Mary's purification were ended, Joseph and Mary carried Him from Bethlehem to Jerusalem to present Him to the Lord in the temple. The Lord of the temple was entering the temple of the Lord, but few visitors there could have been less noticed by the priests, for Mary, instead of offering the sacrifice that was usual in such cases, could only afford two turtledoves, the offering of the poor (Luke 2:24).

However, there were eyes looking on, undazzled by the shows and glitter of the world, from which His poverty could not conceal Him. Simeon, an aged saint, who in answer to many prayers had received a secret promise that he would not die until he had seen the Messiah, met the parents and the child. Suddenly it shot through him like a flash of lightning that this at last was He, and taking Him up in his arms, he praised God for the coming of the One who would bring light to the gentiles and who was the glory of His people Israel (Isaiah 42:6; Luke 2:32).

While Simeon was still speaking, another witness joined the group. It was Anna, a saintly widow who literally dwelt in the courts of the Lord. She had purified the eye of her spirit with the healing salves and herbs of prayer and fasting until it could pierce the veils of the senses with a prophetic glance. She united her testimony to that of Simeon, praising God and confirming the mighty secret to the other expectant souls who were hoping for redemption in Israel.

The shepherds and these aged saints were near the location where the new force entered the world, but it also thrilled receptive souls at a much greater distance. It was probably after the presentation in the temple and after the parents had carried their child back to Bethlehem, where it was their intention to reside instead of returning to Nazareth, that He was visited by the wise men of the East (Matthew 2:1-12). These were members of the educated class of the Magians, the storehouses of science, philosophy, medical skill, and religious mysteries in the countries beyond the Euphrates. Tacitus, Suetonius, and Josephus tell us that in the regions from where they came, there then prevailed an expectation that a great king was to arise in Judea. We know also from the calculations of the great astronomer Kepler that at this very time there was visible in the heavens a brilliant temporary star.

The magi were enthusiastic students of astrology who believed that any unusual phenomenon in the heavens was the sign of some remarkable event on earth. It is possible that, connecting this star, to which their attention would undoubtedly have been eagerly directed, with the expectation mentioned by the ancient historians, they were led westward to see if it had been fulfilled.

There must also have been awakened in them a deeper desire, to which God responded. If their search began in scientific curiosity and speculation, God led it on to the perfect truth. That is always His way. Instead of making tirades against the imperfect, He speaks to us in the language we understand, even if it expresses His meaning very imperfectly, and guides us thereby to the perfect truth.

Just as He used astrology to lead the world to astronomy, and alchemy to conduct it to chemistry, and as the revival of learning during the Renaissance preceded the Reformation, so He used the knowledge of these men, which was half falsehood and superstition, to lead them to the Light of the World. Their visit was a prophecy of how in the future the gentile world would honor His doctrine and salvation, bringing its wealth and talents, its science and philosophy, to offer at His feet.

The shepherds with their simple wonder, Simeon and Anna with a reverence enriched by the treasured wisdom and piety of centuries, and the magi with the lavish gifts of the Orient and the open brow of gentile knowledge all gathered around His cradle to worship the Holy Child. However, while these worthy worshippers were gazing down on Him, a sinister and murderous face came and looked over their shoulders. It was the face of Herod.[2] This prince then occupied the throne of the country, the throne of David and the Maccabees, but he was an alien and low-born usurper. His subjects hated him, and it was only by Roman favor that he was maintained in his seat. He was able, ambitious, and magnificent, yet he had a very cruel, crafty, gloomy, and filthy mind. He had been guilty of every crime. He had made his very palace swim in blood, having murdered his favorite wife, three of his sons, and many of his other relatives.

He was now old and tortured with disease and grief. He was unpopular and was a cruel terror to every possible candidate to the throne that he had usurped. The magi had naturally turned their steps to the capital in order to inquire where He was to be born whose sign they had seen in the East. The thought touched Herod in his sorest place, but with diabolical hypocrisy he concealed his suspicions. Having learned from the priests that the Messiah was to be born in Bethlehem, he directed the strangers there, but arranged for them to return and tell him the very house where the new King was. He hoped to cut Him off with a single blow.

However, his plans were frustrated, for being warned by God, the wise men did not return to tell Herod, but returned to their own country another way. Herod's fury then burst forth like

---

2   The Herods of the New Testament:
    i.   Herod the Great, in whose reign Jesus was born, reigned over the whole of Israel; died very soon after Jesus' birth; his kingdom was divided at his death among his sons.
    ii.   Herod Antipas, son of the former, was at his father's death made tetrarch of Galilee and Perea; the murderer of the Baptist; Jesus was sent to him by Pilate.
    iii.   Herod Agrippa I, grandson of Herod the Great, had as great dominions as he; put James to death and imprisoned Peter; died miserably, as is related in Acts 12.
    iv.   Herod Agrippa II, son of Agrippa I; Paul appeared before him, Acts 25.

a storm, and he sent his soldiers to murder every child under two years of age in Bethlehem (Matthew 2:16-18). He just as well could have attempted to cut through a mountain of stone as to cut the chain of the divine purposes.

He thrust his sword into the nest, but the bird had already flown. Joseph had fled with the Child to Egypt, remaining there until Herod died, when he returned and dwelt at Nazareth. Joseph had been warned not to return to Bethlehem because he would have been there in the kingdom of Archelaus, the like-minded son of a bloodthirsty father (Matthew 2:19-23). Herod's murderous face, glaring down on the Infant, was a sad prophecy of how the powers of the world were to persecute Him and cut off His life from the earth.

The Silent Years at Nazareth

The records that we possess about Jesus up to this point are, as we have seen, comparatively full. But after moving to Nazareth after the return from Egypt, our information comes to a sudden stop. Regarding the rest of the life of Jesus up until His public ministry begins, a thick covering is drawn that is only lifted once. We would have wanted the information to continue with the same fullness through the years of His boyhood and youth.

In modern biographies, few parts are more interesting than the anecdotes that are told of the childhood of the subject, for in these we can often see in miniature and in charming simplicity the character and the plan of the future life. What would we give to know the habits, the friendships, the thoughts, the words, and the actions of Jesus during these early years? Only one flower of anecdote has been thrown over the wall of the hidden garden, and it is so exquisite that it fills us with intense longing to see the garden itself. However, it has pleased God, whose silence is no less wonderful than His words, to keep it closed to us.

It was natural that where God was silent and curiosity was strong, the imagination of man would attempt to fill up the blank. Accordingly, in the early church there appeared apocryphal gospels that pretended to give full details where the inspired Gospels were silent. They are particularly full of the sayings and activities of the childhood of Jesus, but they only show how unequal the human imagination was to such a theme. Their glitter and imaginative depictions contrast with the solidity and truthfulness of the Scripture narrative. They make Him a worker of frivolous and useless marvels, such as molding birds of clay and making them fly, changing His playmates into young goats, and so forth. Basically, they are compilations of worthless and often blasphemous fables.

These absurd failures warn us not to allow the suggestions of imagination to intrude into the hallowed enclosure. It is enough to know that He grew *in wisdom and stature, and in favor with God and man* (Luke 2:52). He was a real child and youth, and He passed through all the stages of natural development. Body and mind grew together, the one expanding to manly vigor, and the other acquiring more and more knowledge and power. His opening character exhibited a grace that made everyone who saw it wonder and love its goodness and purity.

Although we are forbidden to allow our imaginations to run loose here, it is our duty to make use of such authentic materials as are supplied by the manners and customs of the time, or by incidents of His later life that refer back to His earlier years, in order to connect His infancy with the period when the Gospel narratives again take up the thread of biography. It is possible in this way to gain, at least in some degree, an idea of what Jesus was like as a boy and a young man, as well as what the influences were amid which His development proceeded through so many silent years.

We know the kind of home influences in which He was brought up. His home was one of those that were the glory of

His country, as they are of our own – the homes of the godly and intelligent working class. Joseph, its head, was a godly and wise man, but the fact that he is not mentioned in Christ's later life has generally been believed to indicate that he died during the youth of Jesus, perhaps leaving the care of the household on His shoulders.

His mother probably exercised the most decisive of all external influences on His development. What she was can be inferred from the fact that she was chosen from all the women of the world to be crowned with the supreme honor of womanhood. The song that she poured forth on the subject of her own great destiny shows her to have been a woman devoted to God and fervently poetical (Luke 1:46-55). She was a student of Scripture, and especially of its great women, for her song is saturated with Old Testament ideas and is built upon Hannah's song (1 Samuel 2:1-10). Mary has a spirit that is exquisitely humble, yet capable of thoroughly appreciating the honor conferred upon her. She was not the miraculous queen of heaven, as superstition has caricatured her, but was a woman exquisitely pure, holy, loving, and honorable. This is aureole (halo) enough. Jesus grew up in her love and passionately returned it.

There were other residents of the household. Jesus had brothers and sisters. From two of these, James and Jude, we have epistles in Holy Scripture in which we learn from them. It is likely, in their unbelieving state, that they were somewhat harsh and unsympathetic men. In any event, they seemed to have not believed on Him during His lifetime, and it is not likely that they were close companions to Him in Nazareth (John 7:3-5).

Jesus was probably much alone, and the sentiment behind His saying, that a prophet is not without honor except in his own country and in his own house, probably reached back into the years before His ministry began (Matthew 13:57; Mark 6:4).

He received His education at home, or from a scribe attached to the village synagogue. It was only, however, a poor man's education. As the scribes contemptuously said, He had never learned, or as we would say, He was not college-bred. Maybe not, but the love of knowledge was awake within Him early (John 7:15). He knew daily the joy of deep and happy thought. He had the best of all keys to knowledge – an open mind and a loving heart – and He had the three great books always open before Him – the Bible, man, and nature.

It is easy to understand with what fervent intensity Jesus would devote Himself to the Old Testament. His sayings, which are full of quotations from it, provide abundant proof of how constantly it formed the food of His mind and the comfort of His soul. His youthful study of it was the secret of the marvelous ability with which He made use of it afterward in order to enrich His preaching, enforce His doctrine, repel the assaults of opponents, and overcome the temptations of the Evil One.

His quotations also show that He read it in the original Hebrew, and not in the Greek translation that was then in general use. Hebrew was a dead language even in Israel, just as Latin now is in Italy, but Jesus would naturally want to read it in the very words in which it was written. Those who have not enjoyed a broad education, but amid many difficulties have mastered Greek in order to read their New Testament in the original language, will perhaps best understand how, in a country village, Jesus made Himself master of the ancient tongue, and with what delight He was accustomed, in the scrolls of the synagogue or in such manuscripts as He may have Himself possessed, to carefully read over the sacred page.

The language in which He thought and spoke familiarly was Aramaic, a branch of the same stem to which the Hebrew language belongs. We have fragments of it in some recorded sayings of His, such as *Talitha, cumi* (Mark 5:41) and *Eloi, Eloi, lama sabachthani* (Mark 15:34). He would have the same chance of learning Greek as a boy born in the Scottish Highlands has of learning English, since the *Galilee of the Gentiles* (Matthew 4:15) was then full of Greek-speaking inhabitants.

Therefore, Jesus probably mastered three languages. One of them was the grand religious language of the world in whose literature He was deeply versed. Another was the most perfect means of expressing secular thought that has ever existed, although there is no evidence that He had any acquaintance with the masterpieces of Greek literature. The third was the language of the common people to whom His preaching was to be especially addressed.

There are few places where human nature can be better studied than in a country village, for there one sees the whole of each individual life and knows one's neighbors thoroughly. Far more people are seen in a city, but far fewer of the people are known. It is only the outside of life that is visible. In a village, though, the view outward is limited, but the view downward is deep and the view upward is unimpeded.

Nazareth was a notoriously wicked town, as we learn from the proverbial question, *Can any good thing come out of Nazareth?* (John 1:46). Jesus had no acquaintance with sin in His own soul, but in the town He had a full exhibition of the awful problem that it was to be His life's work to deal with.

He was still further brought into contact with human nature by His trade. There can be no doubt that He worked as a carpenter in Joseph's shop. Who could know better than His own townsmen, who asked, in their astonishment at His preaching, *Is not this the carpenter?* (Mark 6:3). It would be difficult to exhaust the significance of the fact that God chose for His Son, when He dwelt among men, out of all the possible positions in which He might have placed Him, the part of a working man. It stamped men's common toils with everlasting honor. It acquainted Jesus with the feelings of the multitude, and it helped Him to know what was in man. It was later said that He knew this so well that He did not need anyone to teach Him (1 John 2:27).

Travelers tell us that the spot where Jesus grew up is one of the most beautiful places on the face of the earth. Nazareth is situated in a secluded, cup-like valley amid the mountains of Zebulon, right where they dip down into the Plain of Esdraelon, with which it is connected by a steep and rocky path. Its white houses, with vines clinging to their walls, are enclosed amid gardens and groves of olive, fig, orange, and pomegranate trees. The fields are divided by hedges of cactus and are enameled with innumerable flowers of every hue.

Behind the village rises a hill five hundred feet high, from whose summit is seen one of the most wonderful views in the world. The mountains of Galilee, with snowy Hermon towering above them, are on the north. The ridge of Carmel, the coast of Tyre, and the sparkling waters of the Mediterranean are on the west. A few miles to the east are the wooded, cone-like bulk of Tabor. To the south is the Plain of Esdraelon, with the mountains of Ephraim beyond.

The preaching of Jesus shows how deeply He had drunk the essence of natural beauty and reveled in the changing aspects of the seasons. It was when wandering in these fields as a lad that He gathered the images of beauty that He poured out in His parables and addresses. It was on that hill that He acquired the habit of retreating to the mountaintops to spend the night in solitary prayer. The doctrines of His preaching were not thought out on the spur of the moment – they were poured out in a living stream when the occasion came – but the water had been gathered into the hidden well for many years before. In the fields and on the mountainside, He had thought them out during the years of happy and undisturbed meditation and prayer.

There is still one important educational influence to be mentioned. Every year after He was twelve years old, He went with His parents to the Passover at Jerusalem. Fortunately, an account has been preserved of the first of these visits. It is the only occasion on which the veil is lifted during thirty years. Everyone who can remember his own first journey from a village home to the capital of his country will understand the joy and excitement with which Jesus set out.

He traveled over eighty miles of a country where nearly every mile teemed with historical and inspiring memories. He mingled with the constantly growing caravan of pilgrims who were filled with the religious enthusiasm of the great ecclesiastical event of the year. His destination was a city that was loved by every Jewish heart with a strength of affection that has never been given to any other capital. It was a city full of objects and memories suited to touch the deepest springs of interest and emotion in His heart.

It was swarming at the time of Passover with strangers from about fifty different countries, speaking as many languages and wearing as many different types of clothing. For the first time, Jesus was to take part in an ancient ceremony suggestive of countless patriotic and sacred memories. It is no wonder that, when the day came to return home, He was so excited with the new objects of interest that He failed to join His party at the appointed place and time.

One place above all others fascinated His interest. It was the temple, and especially the school there in which the masters of wisdom taught. His mind was full of questions that these doctors might be asked to answer. His thirst for knowledge had an opportunity for the first time to drink its fill. It was there that His anxious parents who, missing Him after a day's journey northward, returned in anxiety to seek Him, and found Him listening with excited looks to the oracles of the wisdom of the day. His answer to the reproachful question of His mother lays bare His childhood's mind, and for a moment offers a wide glance over the thoughts that used to preoccupy Him in the fields of Nazareth (Luke 2:41-52).

It has often been asked whether Jesus knew all along that He was the Messiah, and if not, when and how the knowledge dawned upon Him. Was it suggested by hearing the story of His birth from His mother, or was it announced to Him from within? Did it dawn upon Him all at once or gradually? When did the plan of His career, which He carried out so unhesitatingly from the beginning of His ministry, shape itself in His mind? Was it the slow result of years of reflection, or did it come to Him at once? These questions have occupied the greatest Christian minds and have received very various answers. I will not try to answer them, and especially with His reply to His mother before me (Luke 2:49), I cannot trust myself even to think of a time when He did not know what His work in this world was to be.

His subsequent visits to Jerusalem must have greatly influenced the development of His mind. If He often went back to hear and question the rabbis in the temple schools, He must soon have discovered how shallow their far-famed learning was. It was probably on these annual visits that He discovered the utter corruption of the religion of the day and the need for a radical reform of both doctrine and practice, and also indicated the people and practices that He was later to assail with the vehemence of His holy indignation.

These were the external conditions amid which the manhood of Jesus grew toward maturity. It would be easy to exaggerate the influence that they might have exerted on His development. The greater and more original a character is, the less dependent it is on the characteristics of its environment. It is fed from deep wellsprings within itself, and in its beginning there is a type enclosed that expands in obedience to its own laws and bids defiance to circumstances. In any other circumstances, Jesus would have grown to be in every important respect the very same person as He became in Nazareth.

Chapter 2

The Nation and the Time

W e now approach the time when, after thirty years of silence and obscurity in Nazareth, Jesus was to step forth on the public stage. This is, therefore, the point at which to take a survey of the circumstances of the nation in whose midst His work was to be done, and also to form a clear conception of His character and aims.

Every great biography is a record of the entrance into the world of a new force, bringing with it something different from all that was there before, and of the way in which it gradually gets itself incorporated with the old so as to become a part of the future. Obviously, therefore, two things are needed by those who want to understand it: first, a clear comprehension of the nature of the new force itself, and secondly, a view of the world with which it is to be incorporated. Without the latter, the specific difference of the former cannot be understood, nor can the manner of its reception be appreciated, such as the welcome with which it is received or the opposition with which it has to struggle.

Jesus brought with Him into the world more that was original and destined to modify the future history of mankind than anyone else who has ever entered it. However, we can neither understand Him nor the circumstances that He encountered in seeking to incorporate with history the gifts He brought without a clear view of the condition of the sphere within which His life was to be passed.

The Setting of His Life

When we finish the last chapter of the Old Testament and turn the page and see the first chapter of the New, we are very likely to think that we are still among the same people and the same state of things in Matthew that we have left in Malachi. However, that idea would not be true. Four centuries had passed between Malachi and Matthew and had brought about as thorough of a change in Israel as a period of the same length would bring about in any country. The very language of the people had been changed, and customs, ideas, groups, and institutions had come into existence that would almost have prevented Malachi, if he had risen from the dead, from recognizing his country.

Politically, the nation had passed through extraordinary changes. After the exile, it had been organized as a kind of sacred state under its high priests, but conqueror after conqueror had since marched over it, changing everything. The old hereditary monarchy had been restored for a time by the brave Maccabees. The battle of freedom had been won and lost many times. A usurper had sat on the throne of David, and now at last the country was completely under the mighty Roman power, which had extended its sway over the whole civilized world.

It was divided into several small portions, which the foreigner held under different administrations, just as the English used to hold India. Galilee and Perea were ruled by petty kings, sons of that Herod under whom Jesus was born, who occupied a relation to the Roman emperor similar to that which the subject Indian kings held to the English king. Judea was under the charge of a Roman official, a subordinate of the governor of the Roman province of Syria.

Roman soldiers paraded through the streets of Jerusalem. Roman banners waved over the structures of the country. Roman tax-gatherers sat at the gate of every town. To the Sanhedrin, the supreme Jewish agency of government, only a shadow of power was still conceded. Its presidents, the high priests, were mere puppets of Rome, set up and put down at the slightest impulse. The proud nation, whose ideal it had been to rule the world and whose patriotism was a religious and national passion as intense and unquenchable as ever burned in any country, had fallen low.

The changes in religion had been equally great, and the fall had been equally low. In external appearance, indeed, it might have seemed as if progress had been made instead of decline. The nation was far more orthodox than it had been at many earlier periods of its history. Its main danger had once been idolatry, but the chastisement of the exile had corrected that tendency forever, and from then on, the Jews, wherever they were living, were uncompromising monotheists.

The priestly orders and offices had been thoroughly reorganized after the return from Babylon, and the temple services and annual feasts continued to be observed at Jerusalem with strict regularity. Besides, a new and most important religious institution had arisen that almost threw the temple and its priesthood into the background. This was the synagogue with its rabbis. It does not seem to have existed in ancient times at all, but was called into existence after the exile by reverence for the written Word. Synagogues were multiplied wherever Jews lived. Every Sabbath they were filled with praying congregations. Exhortations were delivered by the rabbis – a new order of men created by the need for teachers to translate from Hebrew, which had become a dead language. Nearly the entire Old Testament was read over once a year in the hearing of the people. Schools of theology, similar to our divinity halls, had sprung up, in which the rabbis were trained and the sacred books interpreted.

Despite all this religiousness, though, religion had sadly declined. The externals had been multiplied, but the inner spirit had disappeared. However crude and sinful the old nation had sometimes been, it was capable in its worst periods of producing majestic religious figures who kept high the ideal of life and preserved the connection of the nation with heaven, and the inspired voices of the prophets kept the stream of truth running fresh and clean.

However, during four hundred years, no prophet's voice had been heard. The records of the old prophetic utterances were still preserved with almost idolatrous reverence, but there were not men with even the necessary amount of the Spirit's inspiration to understand what He had previously written.

The representative religious men of the time were the Pharisees. As their name (meaning *separated*) indicates, they originally arose as champions of the separateness of the Jews from other nations. This was a noble idea, as long as the distinction emphasized was holiness. However, it is far more difficult to maintain this distinction than such external differences as distinctness of clothing, food, language, etc. Over time, these things were substituted for holiness.

The Pharisees were impassioned patriots, always willing to lay down their lives for the independence of their country, and they hated the foreign yoke with zealous bitterness. They despised and hated other races and clung with undying faith to the hope of a glorious future for their nation. They had so long repeated this idea that they had come to believe that they were themselves the special favorites of heaven simply because they were descendants of Abraham, and they lost sight of the importance of personal character. They multiplied their Jewish distinctiveness, but they substituted external observances such as fasts, prayers, tithes, washings, sacrifices, and so forth for the grand distinctions of love to God and love to man.

Most of the scribes belonged to the Pharisaic party. They were so called because they were both the interpreters and copyists of the Scriptures and the lawyers of the people, for since the Jewish legal code was incorporated in the Holy Scriptures, jurisprudence became a branch of theology. They were the chief interpreters in the synagogues, although any male worshipper was permitted to speak if he chose. They professed absolute reverence for the Scriptures, counting every word and letter in them. They had a splendid opportunity of imparting the religious principles of the Old Testament among the people, exhibiting the glorious examples of its heroes and sowing abroad the words of the prophets, for the synagogue was one of the most effective methods of instruction ever devised by any people – but they entirely missed their opportunity.

They became a dry ecclesiastical and scholastic class, using their position for selfish exaltation, and scorning those to whom they gave stones for bread as a low and unlettered population. They passed over whatever was most spiritual, living, human, and grand in the Scriptures. Generation after generation, the commentaries of their famous men multiplied, and the students studied the commentaries instead of the text. Moreover, it was a rule with them that the correct interpretation of a passage was as authoritative as the text itself. The interpretations of the famous masters were automatically believed to be correct, and so the large volume of opinions that were held to be as precious as the Bible itself grew to enormous proportions. These were *the traditions of the elders* (Matthew 15:2; Mark 7:3).

By degrees, an arbitrary system of exegesis became popular by which almost any opinion whatsoever could be connected with some text and stamped with divine authority. Every new invention of Pharisaic peculiarity was approved in this way. Peculiarities were multiplied until they regulated every detail of personal, domestic, social, and public life. They became so numerous that it required a lifetime to learn them all. The learning of a scribe consisted in becoming acquainted with them, along with the statements of the great rabbis and the forms of exegesis by which they were sanctioned.

This was the chaff with which they fed the people in the synagogues. The conscience was burdened with innumerable details, every one of which was represented to be as divinely sanctioned as any of the Ten Commandments. This was the unbearable burden that Peter said neither he nor his fathers had been able to bear (Acts 15:10). This was the horrible nightmare that sat so long on Paul's conscience, but worse consequences flowed from it.

It is a well-known principle in history that whenever the ceremonial is elevated to the same rank as the moral, the latter will soon be lost sight of. The scribes and Pharisees had learned how, by inconsistent exegesis and misleading discussion, to explain away the most serious moral obligations and make up for the neglect of them by multiplying ritual observances. Thus, people were able to parade in the pride of sanctity while indulging their selfishness and sinful passions. Society was rotten with wickedness within and was covered over with a self-deceptive religiousness without.

There was a party of protest. The Sadducees challenged the authority attached to the traditions of the fathers, demanding a return to the Bible and nothing but the Bible. They cried out for morality in place of ritual. However, their protest was prompted merely by the spirit of denial rather than by a warm opposite principle of religion.

They were skeptical, cold-hearted, worldly men. Although they praised morality, it was a morality unwarmed and unilluminated by any contact with that upper region of divine forces from which the inspiration of the highest morality must always come. The Sadducees refused to burden their consciences with the painful formalities and regulations of the Pharisees, but it was because they wanted to live a life of comfort and self-indulgence.

They ridiculed the Pharisaic exclusivity, but they had let go of what was most distinctive in the character, the faith, and the hopes of the nation. They mingled freely with the gentiles, affected Greek culture, enjoyed foreign amusements, and thought it useless to fight for the freedom of their country. An extreme branch of them were the Herodians, who had yielded to the usurpation of Herod, and with courtly flattery attached themselves to the favor of his sons.

The Sadducees belonged mainly to the upper and wealthy classes. The Pharisees and scribes formed what we would call the middle class, although also deriving many members from the higher ranks of life. The lower classes and the country people were separated by a great gulf from their wealthy neighbors, but they attached themselves by admiration to the Pharisees, as the uneducated always do to the party of emotions. Down below all these was a large class of those who had lost all connection with religion and well-ordered social life – the publicans, prostitutes, and sinners – for whose souls no one cared.

Such were the lamentable features of the society on which Jesus was about to discharge His influence. Israel was a nation enslaved. The upper classes devoted themselves to selfishness, flattery, and skepticism. The teachers and main professors of religion were lost in mere shows of ceremonialism, boasting that they were the favorites of God while their souls were filled with self-deception and sin. The majority of the people were misled by false ideals, and seething at the bottom of society was a neglected mass of those indulged in shameless and unrestrained sin.

And this was the people of God! Yes, despite their dreadful degradation, these were the children of Abraham, Isaac, and Jacob. These were the heirs of the covenant and the promises.

Towering far back beyond the centuries of degradation were the figures of the patriarchs, the kings after God's own heart, the psalmists, the prophets, and the generations of faith and hope. Yes, and there was greatness in front, too! Once the Word of God is sent forth from heaven and uttered by the mouths of His prophets, it cannot return to Him void (Isaiah 55:11).

God had said that the perfect revelation of Himself was to be given to this nation, that in it was to appear the perfect ideal of manhood, and that from it was to issue forth the regeneration of all mankind. Therefore, a wonderful future still belonged to it. The river of Jewish history was for the time choked and lost in the sands of the desert, but it was destined to reappear again and flow forward on its God-appointed course. The time of fulfillment was at hand, although the signs of the times might have seemed to forbid the hope. Had not all the prophets from Moses onward spoken of a Great One to come, who, appearing just when the darkness was blackest and the degradation deepest, was to bring back the lost glory of the past?

More than a few faithful souls asked themselves that question during this weary and debased time. There are good people in the worst of times. There were good people even in the selfish and corrupt Jewish parties. Piety especially lingers in such times in the humble homes of the people. Just as we are permitted to hope that in the Roman Catholic Church at the present time there may be those who reach out to Christ despite all the ceremonies put between Him and the soul, and by the selection of a spiritual instinct seize the truth and pass by the falsehood, so among the common people of Israel there were those who, hearing the Scriptures read in the synagogues and reading them in their homes, instinctively neglected the cumbersome and endless comments of their teachers and saw the glory of the past, of holiness, and of God that the scribes failed to see.

It was especially to the promises of a Deliverer that such

people focused their interest. Feeling bitterly the shame of national slavery, the hollowness of the times, and the awful wickedness that rotted under the surface of society, they longed and prayed for the advent of the coming One and the restoration of the national character and glory.

The scribes also busied themselves with this aspect of the Scriptures, and cherishing messianic hopes was one of their main distinctions from the Pharisees. However, they had distorted the prophetic utterances on the subject by their inconsistent interpretations, and they painted the future in colors borrowed from their own worldly imaginations.

They spoke of the advent as the coming of the kingdom of God, and they spoke of the Messiah as the Son of God, but what they mainly expected Him to do, by the working of miracles and by an irresistible force, was to free the nation from servitude and raise it to the utmost worldly greatness. They had no doubt that, simply because they were members of the chosen nation, they would be given high places in the kingdom. They never suspected that any change was needed in themselves to meet Him. The more spiritual elements of eternity, holiness, and love were lost in their minds, clouded behind the bright light of earthly glory.

Such was the aspect of Jewish history at the time when the hour of realizing the national destiny was about to strike. It gave a special complexity to the work that lay before the Messiah. It might have been expected that He would find a nation saturated with the ideas and inspired with the visions of His predecessors, the prophets, at whose head He might place Himself, and from which He might receive an enthusiastic and effective cooperation. However, this was not so.

He appeared at a time when the nation had wandered from their ideals and distorted their most noble features. Instead of meeting a nation mature in holiness and consecrated to the heaven-ordained task of blessing all other peoples, which He then could have easily led up to its own final development and then led forth to the spiritual conquest of the world, He found that the first work that lay before Him was to proclaim a reformation in His own country and to encounter the opposition of prejudices that had accumulated there through centuries of degradation.

Chapter 3

The Final Stages of His Preparation

M eanwhile, the Messiah, whom so many in their own way were hoping for, was in the midst of them, although they did not suspect it. Little could they think that He, about whom they were speculating and praying, was growing up in a carpenter's home in despised Nazareth, yet it was so. He was there preparing Himself for His career. His mind was busy grasping the vast proportions of the task before Him, as the prophecies of the past and the facts of the case determined it. His eyes were looking forth on the country, and His heart was aching with the sense of its sin and shame. He felt the gigantic powers necessary to cope with the immense task moving within Him. The desire was gradually growing to an irresistible passion to go forth and proclaim the thought within Him and do the work that He had been given to do.

Jesus only had three years to accomplish His lifework. If we remember how quickly three years in an ordinary life pass by, and how little at their end there usually is to show for them, we will see what the size and quality of that character must have been, and what unity and intensity of design there was in that life that in such a marvelously short time made such a deep and enduring impression on the world and left to mankind such a heritage of truth and influence.

It is generally agreed that Jesus appeared as a public man with a mind whose ideas were completely developed and arranged, with a character sharpened over its whole surface into perfect precision, and with intent and purpose that marched forward to their ends without hesitation. No deviation took place during the three years from the course on which He was headed. The reason for this must have been that during the thirty years before His public work began, His ideas, His character, and purposes went through all the stages of a thorough development.

As unpretentious as the external aspects of His life at Nazareth were, below the surface it was a life of intensity, variety, and dignity. Beneath the silence and obscurity, there occurred all the processes of growth that resulted in the magnificent flower and fruit to which all ages now look back with wonder.

His preparation lasted long. For someone with the powers at His command, thirty years of complete restraint and reserve were a long time. Nothing was greater in Him afterward than the majestic reserve in both speech and action that characterized Him. This, too, was learned in Nazareth. He waited there until the hour of the completion of His preparation struck. Nothing could tempt Him to begin before the time – not the burning desire to interfere with indignant protest amid the crying corruptions and mistakes of the age, and not even the continued increase of the passion to do His fellow-men good.

At last, however, He threw down the carpenter's tools, laid aside the workman's clothing, and said farewell to His home and the beloved valley of Nazareth. Still, however, all was not ready. His manhood, though it had grown in secret to such noble proportions, still required a special endowment for the work He had to do. His ideas and plans, as prepared as they were, had to be hardened in the fire of a momentous trial. The two final incidents of His preparation – the baptism and the temptation – still had to take place.

His Baptism

Jesus did not descend on the nation from the obscurity of Nazareth without a note of warning. His work may be said to have begun before He Himself put His hand to it.

Once more, before hearing the voice of its Messiah, the nation was to hear the long-silent voice of prophecy. The news went through all the country that a preacher had appeared in the desert of Judea. He was not like the mumblers of dead men's ideas who spoke in the synagogues, or the flattering, smooth-tongued teachers of Jerusalem, but he was a rude, strong man, speaking from the heart to the heart, with the authority of one who was sure of his inspiration. He had been a Nazarite from the womb. He had lived for years in the desert, wandering, in communion with his own heart, beside the lonely shores of the Dead Sea. He was clothed in the garment of hair and leather girdle of the old prophets. His ascetic rigor sought no finer fare than locusts and the wild honey that he found in the wilderness.

Yet he knew life well. He was acquainted with all the evils of the time. He was familiar with the hypocrisy of the religious parties and the corruption of the people. He had a wonderful power of searching the heart and shaking the conscience, and he laid bare the cherished sins of every class without fear.

However, that which most of all attracted attention to him and thrilled every Jewish heart from one end of the land to the other was the message that he proclaimed. It was nothing less than that the Messiah was at hand and was about to set up the kingdom of God. All of Jerusalem swarmed out to him. The Pharisees were eager to hear the messianic news, and even the Sadducees were momentarily stirred from their lethargy. The provinces sent forth their thousands to his preaching, and the scattered and hidden ones who longed and prayed for the redemption of Israel flocked to welcome the heart-stirring promise.

Along with it, though, John had another message that excited very different feelings in different minds. He had to tell his hearers that the nation as a whole was utterly unprepared for the Messiah. He told them that the mere fact of their descent from Abraham would not be sufficient evidence of admission to His kingdom, that it was to be a kingdom of righteousness and holiness, and that Christ's very first work would be to reject all who were not marked with these qualities, just as the farmer winnows away the chaff with his fan and the master of the vineyard cuts down every tree that does not bring forth any fruit.

Therefore this man, John the Baptist, called the nation at large – every class and every individual – to repentance, as long as there was still time, as an indispensable preparation for enjoying the blessings of the new era. As an outward symbol of this inward change, he baptized in the Jordan River all who received his message with faith. Many were stirred with fear and hope and submitted to the practice, but many more were irritated by the exposure of their sins and turned away in anger and unbelief. Among these were the Pharisees, upon whom John the Baptist was especially severe, and who were deeply offended because he had treated their descent from Abraham so lightly, on which they laid so much stress (Luke 3:7-9).

One day there appeared among the Baptist's hearers One who particularly attracted his attention and made his voice, which had never faltered when accusing in the most vigorous language of reproof even the highest teachers and priests of the nation, tremble with self-distrust. When He presented Himself, after the discussion was over, among the candidates for baptism, John hesitated, feeling that this Man was not one in need of the bath of repentance.

John had without hesitation administered this baptism to all others, but thought that he himself had no right to baptize the Messiah. There was in His face a majesty, a purity, and a peace that struck the man of rock with a sense of unworthiness and sin. It was Jesus, who had come straight here from the workshop of Nazareth.

John and Jesus seem never to have met before, although their families were related and the connection of their careers had been predicted before their birth. This may have been due to the distance between their homes in Galilee and Judea, and still more to the Baptist's eccentric habits. However, when in obedience to the instruction of Jesus, John proceeded to administer the ritual, he learned the meaning of the overpowering impression that the Stranger had made on him, for the sign was given by which God had instructed him that he was to recognize the Messiah, whose forerunner he was. The Holy Spirit descended on Jesus as He emerged from the water in the attitude of prayer, and the voice of God thunderously pronounced Jesus to be God's beloved Son (Matthew 3:13-17; John 1:32-33).

The impression made on John by the very look of Jesus revealed much more than many words could have done. It revealed when Jesus was about to begin His work, as well as the qualities of the character that had been slowly ripening to full maturity in Nazareth.

The baptism itself had an important significance for Jesus. To the other candidates who underwent the ceremony, it had a double meaning: it signified the abandonment of their old sins and their entrance into the new messianic era. To Jesus, it could not have the former meaning, except insofar as He might have identified Himself with His nation and taken this way of expressing His sense of its need of cleansing. However, it meant that He, too, was now entering through this door into the new era of which He was Himself to be the Author. It expressed His sense that the time had come to leave behind the employments of Nazareth and to devote himself to His unique work.

Still more important was the descent upon Him of the Holy

Spirit. This was neither a meaningless display nor just a sign to John the Baptist. It was the symbol of a special gift then given to qualify Jesus for His work and to crown the long development of His distinct powers. It is a forgotten truth that the manhood of Jesus was dependent on the Holy Spirit from beginning to end. We are apt to think that its connection with His divine nature made this unnecessary. On the contrary, it made it far more necessary, for in order to be the instrument of His divine nature, His human nature had to be both endowed with the highest gifts and constantly sustained in their use.

We are in the habit of attributing the wisdom and grace of His words, His supernatural knowledge of even the thoughts of people, and the miracles He performed, to His divine nature. In the Gospels, though, these are constantly attributed to the Holy Spirit. This does not mean that they were independent of His divine nature, but that in them His human nature was enabled to be the instrument of His divine nature by a special gift of the Holy Spirit. This gift was given to Him at His baptism. It was comparable to the possession of prophets, like Isaiah and Jeremiah, with the Spirit of inspiration on those occasions, of which they have left accounts, when they were called to begin their public life, and to the special outpouring of the same influence still sometimes given at their ordination to those who are about to begin the work of the ministry. To Jesus, though, it was given without measure, while to others it has always been given only in measure, and it especially consisted of the gift of miraculous powers.

The Temptation

An immediate effect of this new gift appears to have been one often experienced, in less degree, by others who have received this same gift of the Spirit for work. His whole being was excited about His work. His desires to be engaged in it were raised to the highest degree. His thoughts were intensely occupied about the means of its accomplishment.

Although His preparation for it had been going on for many years, and although His whole heart had long been focused on it and His plan had been clearly settled, it was natural that when the divine signal had been given that it was time to begin and He felt Himself suddenly put in possession of the supernatural powers necessary for carrying it out, His mind would be in a tumult of rushing thoughts and feelings. It would be natural for Jesus to seek a place of solitude to meditate once again upon the whole situation.

Therefore, He promptly retreated from the bank of the Jordan River, driven, we are told, into the wilderness by the Spirit, who had been given to Him (Mark 1:12). For forty days, Jesus wandered among the sandy dunes and wild mountains, depriving himself of the pleasures of the world and the flesh, instead fasting while resisting the temptations of the devil (Matthew 4:1-11; Luke 4:1-13).

It is with surprise and amazement that we learn that during those days His soul was the scene of a terrible struggle. He was tempted by Satan. What could He be tempted with at a time so sacred? To understand this, we must remember what has been said of the state of the Jewish nation, and especially the nature of the messianic hopes they were holding on to. They expected a Messiah who would work amazing wonders and establish a worldwide empire with Jerusalem as its center, and they had postponed the ideas of righteousness and holiness in order to pursue these. They completely reversed the divine conception of the kingdom, giving precedence to the material and political considerations rather than to the spiritual and moral elements.

In carrying out the great work that His Father had committed to Him, Jesus was tempted to yield in some measure to these expectations. He must have foreseen that the nation would be disappointed and would probably turn away from Him in unbelief and anger unless He did so. The different temptations were only various modifications of this one thought. The suggestion that He should turn stones into bread to satisfy His hunger was a temptation to use the power of working miracles, with which He had been endowed, for a purpose inferior to that for which alone it had been given. This was the precursor of such temptations later in His life as the multitude demanded Him to show them a sign or that He should come down from the cross so they could believe Him (Matthew 27:40; John 6:30).

The suggestion that He should leap from the pinnacle of the temple was probably also a temptation to gratify the crude desire for wonders, for it was a part of the popular belief that the Messiah would appear suddenly and in some marvelous way, such as by jumping from the temple roof into the midst of the crowds assembled below.

The third and greatest temptation, to win the empire of all the kingdoms of the world by an act of worship to the Evil One, was evidently just a symbol of obedience to the universal Jewish idea of the coming kingdom as a vast structure of material force. It was a temptation that every worker for God, weary with the slow progress of goodness, must often feel, and to which even good and earnest people have sometimes given way – to begin at the outside instead of within, to first get a framework of external conformity to religion, and afterward fill it with a reality. It was the temptation to which Mohammed yielded when he used the sword to subdue those whom he was later to make religious, and to which the Jesuits yielded when they baptized the heathen first and evangelized them afterward.

It is with amazement that we think of these suggestions presenting themselves to the holy soul of Jesus. Could He be tempted to distrust God, and even to worship the Evil One? No doubt the temptations were flung from Him as the powerless waves fall broken from the heart of the rock on which they have dashed themselves. However, these temptations pressed in on Him, not only at this time, but often before in the valley of Nazareth, and often afterward, in the intensity and crises of His life. We must remember that it is not a sin to be tempted, but it is only sin to yield to temptation. Indeed, the more absolutely pure a soul is, the more painful will be the point of the temptation as it presses for admission into his heart.

Although the tempter only departed from Jesus for a little while, this was a decisive struggle. Satan was completely beaten back, and his power was broken at its heart. John Milton has indicated this by ending his *Paradise Regained* at this point. Jesus emerged from the wilderness with the plan of His life, which, no doubt, had been formed long before, hardened in the fire of trial.

Nothing is more obvious in His later life than the determination with which He carried it out. Other people, even those who have accomplished the greatest tasks, have sometimes not had a definite plan, but only saw the path to pursue a little at a time as their circumstances changed. Their purposes have been modified by events and the advice of others.

However, Jesus started with His plan perfected, and He never deviated from it by even a hairbreadth. He handled the interference of His mother or His disciples with His plan as unwaveringly as He carried it out through the fiery opposition of open enemies. His plan was to establish the kingdom of God in the hearts of individuals, not relying on the weapons of political and material strength, but only on the power of love and the force of truth.

The Divisions of His Public Ministry

The public ministry of Jesus is generally considered to have lasted three years. Each of these years had unique features of its own. The first year can be called the Year of Obscurity, both because the records of it that we possess are very limited, and because during this year Jesus seems to have been only slowly emerging into public notice. It was spent for the most part in Judea.

The second year was the Year of Public Favor, during which the country had become thoroughly aware of Him, His activity was constant, and His fame rang throughout the length and breadth of the land. It was almost entirely spent in Galilee.

The third year was the Year of Opposition. This is when the public approval subsided. His enemies multiplied and assailed Him with more and more tenacity, and at last He fell victim to their hatred. The first six months of this final year were spent in Galilee, and the last six in other parts of the land.

Thus, the life of the Savior in its external outline resembled that of many reformers and benefactors of mankind. Such a life often begins with a period during which the public is gradually made aware of the new man in its midst. Then it passes into a period when his doctrine or reform is carried high on the shoulders of popularity, and it ends with a reaction, when the old prejudices and interests that have been assailed by him rally from his attack and, gaining to themselves the emotions of the crowd, crush him in their rage.

Chapter 4

The Year of Obscurity

The records of this first year of the ministry of Jesus that we possess are extremely limited, comprising only two or three incidents that can be listed here, especially as they form a kind of program of His future work.

When Jesus emerged from the wilderness after the forty days of temptation with His grasp of His future plan tightened by that dreadful struggle, along with the inspiration of His baptism still filling His heart, He appeared once more on the bank of the Jordan River, and John the Baptist pointed Him out as the great successor to himself of whom he had often spoken. He especially introduced Him to some of the best of his own disciples, who immediately became His followers (John 1:35-42).

Probably the very first of these to whom Jesus spoke was John, the man who was later to be His favorite disciple and who would give to the world the most marvelous portrait of His character and life. John the Evangelist has left an account of this first meeting and the interview that followed it, which retains in all its freshness the impression that Christ's majesty and purity made on his receptive mind.

The other young men who attached themselves to Him at the same time were Andrew, Peter, Philip, and Nathanael. They had been prepared for their new Master by their communication with John the Baptist, and although they did not at once leave their jobs and follow Him in the same way as they did later, they received impressions at their very first meeting that influenced and affected the rest of their lives.

It does not seem that John the Baptist's disciples all began following Christ at once, but the best of them did so. Some troublemakers tried to excite envy in John the Baptist's mind by pointing out how his influence was being transferred to another, but they did not understand that great man, whose main cause of greatness was his humility. He answered them that it was his joy to decrease, while Christ increased, for it was Christ who as the Bridegroom was to lead home the bride, while he was only the Bridegroom's friend, whose happiness consisted in seeing the crown of festive joy placed on the head of another (John 3:25-30).

With His newly attached followers, Jesus departed from the scene of John's ministry and went north to Cana in Galilee to attend a marriage to which He had been invited. Here He made the first display of the miraculous powers with which He had been endowed. He turned water into wine. It was a manifestation of His glory intended especially for His new disciples who, we are told, from then on believed on Him (John 2:1-11).

This means, no doubt, that they were fully convinced that He was the Messiah. It was intended also to strike the keynote of His ministry as being completely different from that of John the Baptist. John was an ascetic hermit who fled from the dwellings of men and called his hearers out into the wilderness. Jesus, though, had glad tidings to bring to people's homes. He was to mingle in their common lives and produce a happy change in their circumstances, which would be like turning the water of their lives into wine.

Soon after this miracle, Jesus returned again to Judea to attend the Passover, where He gave a still more remarkable proof of the joyful and enthusiastic mood in which He was then living by purging the temple of the sellers of animals and the money changers, who had introduced their commerce into its courts (John 2:13-17). These people were allowed to carry on their sacrilegious trade under the pretense of accommodating strangers who came to worship at Jerusalem by selling them the animals that they could not bring from foreign countries. They also supplied, in exchange for foreign money, the Jewish coins in which alone they could pay their temple dues.

However, what had been begun under the veil of a pious pretext had ended in extreme disturbance of the worship and in elbowing the gentile proselytes from the place that God had allowed them in His house. Jesus had probably often witnessed the disgraceful scene with indignation during His visits to Jerusalem, and now, with the prophetic zeal of His baptism upon Him, He broke out against it. The same look of irresistible purity and majesty that had overpowered John when He sought baptism prevented any resistance on the part of the disgraceful group, and it made the onlookers recognize the characteristics of the prophets of ancient days before whom kings and crowds alike were inclined to cower. It was the beginning of His reformatory work against the religious abuses of the time.

Jesus worked other miracles during the feast, which must have excited much talk among the pilgrims from every land who crowded the city. One result was to bring to His lodging one night the respected and concerned inquirer to whom He delivered the marvelous discourse on the nature of the new kingdom He had come to establish, and the way of entering it, which has been preserved to us in the third chapter of John. It seemed to be a hopeful sign that one of the heads of the nation would approach Him in such a humble spirit, but Nicodemus was the only one of them on whose mind the first display of the Messiah's power in the capital produced a deep and favorable impression.

We can clearly follow the first steps of Jesus up to this point, but this is when our information in regard to the first year of His ministry, after beginning with such fullness, comes to a sudden stop. For the next eight months, we learn nothing more about Him except that He was baptizing in Judea, *though Jesus Himself baptized not, but His disciples*, and that He *made and baptized more disciples than John* (John 4:1-2).

What can be the meaning of such a lack of information at this point? It is to be noted, too, that it is only in the fourth Gospel that we receive even the details given above. The Synoptists – Matthew, Mark, and Luke – omit the first year of the ministry completely, beginning their narrative with the ministry in Galilee, and merely indicating in the most casual manner that there was earlier ministry in Judea.

It is very difficult to explain all this. The most natural explanation would probably be that the events of this year were imperfectly known at the time when the Gospels were written. It would be quite natural that the details of the period when Jesus had not attracted much public attention would be much less accurately remembered than those of the period when He was by far the best-known person in the country. While Matthew, Mark, and Luke seem to take little notice of what happened in Judea until the close of His life was near, it is to John that we are indebted for the connected accounts of His various visits to the south.

John could hardly have been ignorant of the incidents of these eight months. We might be drawn to the explanation of the little-noticed fact that John provides – that for a time Jesus took up the work of John the Baptist. He baptized by the hands of His disciples and drew even larger crowds than John. Must not this mean that He was convinced, by the small impression that making Himself known at the Passover had made, that the nation was utterly unprepared for receiving Him yet as the Messiah, and that what was needed was the extension of the preparatory work of repentance and baptism? Therefore, could it not be that, keeping His higher character in the background, He became for the time the colleague of John? This view is confirmed by the fact that it was upon John the Baptist's imprisonment at the end of the year that He fully opened His messianic career in Galilee.

A still deeper explanation of the silence of the Synoptists over this period, along with their meager notice of Christ's later visits to Jerusalem, has been suggested. Jesus came primarily to the Jewish nation, whose authoritative representatives were to be found at Jerusalem. He was the Messiah promised to their fathers. He was the Fulfiller of the nation's history. He indeed had a far wider mission to the whole world, but He was to begin with the Jews, and He was to begin at Jerusalem.

The nation, however, with its leaders at Jerusalem, rejected Him, and so He was compelled to establish His worldwide community somewhere else. This having become evident by the time the Gospels were written, Matthew, Mark, and Luke regarded His activity at the headquarters of the nation as a work that to a great extent had merely negative results. They therefore concentrated their attention on the period of His ministry when He was gathering the company of believing souls that was to form the nucleus of the Christian church.

Whatever the reason, certainly at the end of the first year of the ministry of Jesus, the shadow of a terrible coming event had already fallen over Judea and Jerusalem. It was the shadow of that most offensive of all national crimes that the world has ever witnessed: the rejection and crucifixion by the Jews of their Messiah.

Chapter 5

The Year of Public Favor

After the year spent in the south, Jesus shifted the sphere of His activity to the north part of the country. In Galilee, He would be able to address Himself to minds that were not affected by the preconceptions and arrogant pride of Judea, where the religious and educated classes had their headquarters. Jesus might hope that if His doctrine and influence took a deep hold in one part of the country, even though it was remote from the center of authority, He could return to the south backed with an irresistible national acknowledgment, and could then carry by storm even the citadel of prejudice itself.

Galilee

The area of Jesus' activity for the next eighteen months was very limited. The entire land of Israel was a very limited country. Its length was a hundred miles less than that of Scotland, and its breadth was considerably less than the average breadth of Scotland. It is important to remember this because it helps us understand the swiftness with which the movement of Jesus spread over the land and how all parts of the country flocked to His ministry.

It is interesting to remember it as an illustration of the fact that the nations that have contributed most to the civilization of the world have, during the period of their true greatness, been confined to very small territories. Rome was only a single city, and Greece was a very small country.

Galilee was the most northerly of the four provinces into which Israel was divided. It was sixty miles long and thirty miles wide and consisted for the most part of an elevated plateau whose surface was varied by irregular mountain masses. Near its eastern boundary, it abruptly drops down into a great gulf through which flowed the Jordan River. In the midst of the province of Galilee, at a depth of five hundred feet below the Mediterranean, lay the lovely, harp-shaped Sea of Galilee.

The whole province was very fertile, and the province was densely covered with large villages and towns. The population was about as dense as that of Lancashire or the West Riding of Yorkshire. The center of activity was the basin of the lake, a sheet of water thirteen miles long by six miles wide. Above its eastern shore, around which ran a fringe of green a quarter of a mile wide, there towered high, bare hills that had been cut with the channels of torrents.

On the western side, the mountains were gently sloped and their sides richly cultivated, bearing splendid crops of every description. At the foot of the mountains, the shore was green and rich with luxuriant groves of olives, oranges, figs, and every product of an almost tropical climate.

At the northern end of the lake, the space between the water and the mountains was broadened by the delta of the river, and it was watered with many streams from the hills. It was a perfect paradise of fertility and beauty. It was called the Plain of Gennesaret, and even at this day, when the whole basin of the lake is little better than a parched desert, it is still covered with magnificent cornfields wherever the hand of cultivation touches it. Where idleness leaves it untended, it is overspread with thick jungles of thorn and oleander.

In our Lord's time, it contained the main cities on the lake, such as Capernaum, Bethsaida, and Chorazin, but the whole shore was dotted with towns and villages, and together it formed a perfect beehive of swarming human life. The means of existence were abundant in the crops and fruits of every description that the fields yielded so richly. The waters of the lake were filled with fish, providing employment to thousands of fishermen. Besides, the great highways from Egypt to Damascus, and from Phoenicia to the Euphrates, passed through here and made this a vast center of traffic. Thousands of boats for fishing, transport, and pleasure moved to and fro on the surface of the lake. The whole region was a focus of energy and prosperity.

The report of the miracles that Jesus had performed at Jerusalem eight months earlier had been brought home to Galilee by the pilgrims who had been south at the feast, and doubtless also the news of His preaching and baptism in Judea had created talk and excitement before He arrived. Accordingly, the Galileans were in some measure prepared to receive Him when He returned to their midst.

One of the first places He visited was Nazareth, the home of His childhood and youth. He appeared there one Sabbath in the synagogue, and being now known as a preacher, He was invited to read the Scriptures and address the congregation. He read a passage from Isaiah in which a glowing description is given of the coming and work of the Messiah:

The Spirit of the Lord God is upon me, because He has anointed me to preach the gospel to the poor; He hath sent me to heal the broken-hearted, to preach deliverance to the captives, and recovering of sight to the blind, to set at liberty them that are bruised, to preach the acceptable year of the Lord. (Luke 4:18-19, quoted from Isaiah 61:1-2)

As Jesus commented on this text, picturing the features of

the messianic time – such as emancipating the slave, enriching the poor, and healing the diseased – their curiosity at hearing for the first time a young preacher who had been brought up among them turned into spellbound wonder, and they burst into the applause that used to be allowed in the Jewish synagogues.

Soon, though, the reaction came (Matthew 13:55-58). They began to whisper. Was not this the carpenter who had worked among them? Had not His father and mother been their neighbors? Were not His sisters married in the town? Their envy was excited. When Jesus proceeded to tell them that the prophecy that He had read was fulfilled in Himself, they broke out into angry scorn. They demanded of Him a sign like they had heard He had given in Jerusalem. When He informed them that He could do no miracle among the unbelieving, they rushed against Him in a storm of jealousy and wrath. Hurrying Him out of the synagogue to a cliff behind the town, they would have thrown Him over the cliff if He had not miraculously taken Himself away from them (Luke 4:28-30). He prevented them from crowning their proverbial wickedness with an act that would have robbed Jerusalem of her corrupt fame of being the murderess of the Messiah.

From that day forward, Nazareth was no longer His home. In His tender love for his old neighbors, He visited it once more, but with no better result. From this day forward, He made His home in Capernaum, which is on the northwestern shore of the Sea of Galilee. This town has completely vanished out of existence; its precise location cannot now be identified with any certainty.[3] This might be one reason why it is not connected in the Christian mind with the life of Jesus in the same prominent way as Bethlehem, where He was born; Nazareth, where He was brought up; or Jerusalem, where He died.

We should, though, fix it in our memories side by side with

---

3   The location of Capernaum was not known until British archaeologist Charles Wilson identified the site in 1866. Excavation began at the site in the late 1800s.

these, for it was His home for eighteen of the most important months of His life. It is called His own city, and He was asked for tribute, or tax, in it as a citizen of the place (Matthew 17:24-27). It was thoroughly well adapted to be the center of His labors in Galilee, for it was the focus of the busy life in the basin of the lake, and it was conveniently situated for journeys to all parts of the province. Whatever happened there was quickly heard of in all the regions round about.

In Capernaum, then, Jesus began His Galilean work. For many months, Capernaum was His headquarter from which He traveled in all directions to visit the towns and villages of Galilee. Sometimes His journey would be inland, away to the west. At other times it would be a tour of the villages on the lake, or a visit to the country on its eastern side. He had a boat that waited on Him and was used to take Him wherever He needed to go. He would come back to Capernaum, sometimes only for a day, and sometimes for a week or two at a time.

In a few weeks, the whole province was ringing with His name. He was the topic of conversation in every boat on the lake and in every house in the whole region. People's minds were stirred with great excitement, and everyone desired to see Him. Crowds began to gather around Him. The crowds grew larger and larger. They multiplied to thousands and tens of thousands. They followed Him wherever He went. The news spread far and wide beyond Galilee, bringing people from Jerusalem, Judea, and Perea, and even from Idumaea in the far south and from Tyre and Sidon in the far north. Sometimes He could not stay in any town because the crowds blocked the streets and crowded one another. Jesus had to take them out to the fields and deserts. The country was stirred from end to end, and Galilee was all on fire with excitement about Him.

How was it that He produced such a great and widespread movement? It was not by declaring Himself the Messiah. That would indeed have caused to pass through every Jewish heart the deepest thrill that it could experience. Although Jesus occasionally revealed Himself, as at Nazareth, in general He preferred to conceal who He was.

No doubt the reason for this was that among the excitable crowds of rude Galilee, with their blatant materialistic hopes, the declaration would have excited a revolutionary rising against the Roman government that would have withdrawn people's minds from His true goals and would have brought the Roman sword down upon His head, just as in Judea it would have brought about a murderous attack on His life by the Jewish authorities.

For various reasons, the full revelation of Himself was concealed until the right moment for making it known would come. In the meantime, He would let it be inferred from His character and work who He was.

The two great methods that Jesus used in His work, and which created such attention and enthusiasm, were His miracles and His preaching.

The Miracle Worker

It was likely His miracles that excited the most far-reaching attention. We are told how the news of the first one that He worked in Capernaum spread like wildfire through the town, bringing crowds around the house where He was. Whenever He performed a new miracle of extraordinary character, the excitement grew intense and the news of it spread all over the land.

For example, when Jesus first cured leprosy, the most malignant form of bodily disease in Israel, the amazement of the people knew no limit. It was the same when He first overcame a case of demon possession. When He raised the widow's son to life at Nain, there was a sort of amazed fear followed by delighted wonder and the talk of thousands of people (Luke 7:11-17).

For a time, all Galilee was in motion with the gathering of the diseased of every description who could walk or hobble to be near Him, as well as with groups of concerned friends who carried those who could not come on their own. The streets of the villages and towns were lined with the victims of disease as the gracious Jesus passed by. Sometimes He had so many to attend to that He could not even find time to eat. At one point, He was so absorbed in His benevolent work and so carried along with the resulting holy excitement that His relatives, with coarse indiscretion, attempted to interfere, saying to each other that He was *beside Himself* (Mark 3:21).

The miracles of Jesus, taken altogether, were of two classes: those that were performed on people, and those that were performed in the realm of external nature, such as turning water into wine, calming the storm, and multiplying the loaves. The former were by far the more numerous. They consisted mainly of cures of disease more or less malignant, such as lameness, blindness, deafness, palsy, leprosy, and so forth. Jesus appears to have varied His methods of healing very much, for reasons that we cannot explain. Sometimes He used methods such as a touch, laying moistened clay on the part, or ordering the patient to wash in water. At other times He healed without any means, and occasionally even at a distance.

Besides these bodily cures, He dealt with the diseases of the mind. These seem to have been particularly prevalent in Israel at the time, and they excited intense fear. They were believed to be accompanied by the entrance of demons into the miserable person or delirious victim, and this idea was only too true. The man whom Jesus cured among the tombs in the country of the Gadarenes was a frightful example of this type of disease, and the picture of him sitting at the feet of Jesus clothed and in his right mind shows what an effect His kind, soothing, and authoritative presence has on minds so troubled (Mark 5:2-20; Luke 8:26-39).

The most extraordinary miracles, though, were those that Jesus performed upon man when He raised the dead to life. They were not frequent, but whenever they occurred, they naturally produced an overwhelming impression (e.g., Matthew 9:18-26; Mark 5:22-43; Luke 7:11-17; John 11:1-46).

The miracles of the other class, those of an external nature, were of the same unexplainable kind. Some of His cures of mental disease, if standing by themselves, might be accounted for by the influence of a powerful nature on a troubled mind. In the same way, some of His bodily cures might be accounted for by His influencing the body through the mind. However, a miracle such as walking on the stormy sea (Mark 6:48-49) is completely beyond the reach of natural explanation.

Why did Jesus choose to work miracles? Several answers could be given to this question. First, He worked miracles because His Father gave Him these signs as proof that He had sent Him. Many of the Old Testament prophets had received the same authentication of their mission, and although John the Baptist, who revived the prophetic function, did not work any miracles, as the Gospels inform us with the most simple sincerity (John 10:41), it was to be expected that He who was a far greater prophet than the greatest who went before Him would show even greater signs than any of them of His divine mission. It was an astounding claim that He made on people's faith when He announced Himself as the Messiah, and it would have been unreasonable to expect it to be acknowledged by a nation accustomed to miracles as the signs of a divine mission if He had not performed any.

Secondly, the miracles of Christ were the natural outflow of the divine fullness that dwelt in Him. God was in Him, and His human nature was endowed with the Holy Spirit without measure. It was natural, when such a Being was in the world, that mighty works would manifest themselves in Him. He was Himself the great miracle, and His specific miracles were merely sparks or emanations.

He was the great interruption of the order of nature, or

rather, He was a new element that had entered into the order of nature to enrich and dignify it, and His miracles entered with Him, not to disturb, but to repair its harmony. Therefore, all His miracles bore the stamp of His character. They were not mere demonstrations of power, but were also demonstrations of holiness, wisdom, and love.

The Jews often sought immense signs from Him merely to gratify their thirst for the sensational. Jesus always refused them, though, working only such miracles that were beneficial to faith. He demanded faith in all those whom He cured, and never responded to curiosity or unbelieving challenges to demonstrate His power. This distinguishes His miracles from those fabled of ancient wonder-workers and medieval saints. The miracles of Jesus were marked by constant seriousness and benevolence because they were expressions of His character as a whole.

Thirdly, His miracles were symbols of His spiritual and saving work. It is only necessary to consider them for a moment to see that they were, as a whole, triumphs over the misery of the world. Mankind is the prey of a thousand evils, and even the frame of external nature bears the mark of some past catastrophe: *The whole creation groaneth and travaileth in pain* (Romans 8:22). This huge mess of physical evil in the fate of mankind is the effect of sin. Not every disease and misfortune can be traced to a particular sin, but some of them can.

The consequences of past sins are distributed in detail over the whole human race, yet the misery of the world is the shadow of its sin. Material and moral evil, being closely related, mutually explain each other. When Jesus healed bodily blindness, it was a type of the healing of the inner eye. When He raised the dead, He was suggesting that He was the Resurrection and the Life in the spiritual world as well. When He cleansed the leper, His triumph spoke of victory over the leprosy of sin. When He multiplied the loaves, He followed the miracle by speaking about the bread of life. When He calmed the storm, it was an assurance that He could speak peace to the troubled conscience.

His miracles were a natural and essential part of His messianic work. They were an excellent way to make Him known to the nation. They bound those whom He cured to Him with strong ties of gratitude. Without a doubt, in many cases, faith in Him as a miracle worker led to a higher faith. That is how it was in the case of His devoted follower Mary Magdalene, out of whom He cast seven devils (Mark 16:9).

This work must have brought both great pain and great joy to Jesus. To His tender and lovely sympathetic heart that never grew insensitive in the least degree, it must often have been heartbreaking to mingle with so much disease and see the awful effects of sin. He was in the right place, though, for it suited His great love to be where help was needed.

What a joy it must have been to Him to distribute blessings on every hand, to erase the traces of sin, to see health returning beneath His touch, to meet the joyous and grateful glances of the opening eyes, to hear the blessings of mothers and sisters as He restored their loved ones to their arms, and to see the light of love and welcome in the faces of the poor as He entered their towns and villages. He drank deeply from the well at which He wanted His followers to always be drinking – the delight of doing good.

The Teacher

The other great instrument with which Jesus did His work was His teaching. It was by far the more important of the two. His miracles were only the bell that rang to bring the people to hear His words. They made an impression upon those who might not yet be susceptible to the more delicate influence, and the miracles brought them within its range.

The miracles probably made the most noise, but His preaching also spread His fame far and wide. There is no power whose attraction is more unfailing than that of the eloquent word. Barbarians listening to their poets and storytellers, Greeks listening to the restrained passion of their orators, and matter-of-fact nations like the Roman nation have alike acknowledged the irresistible power of the eloquent word.

The Jews valued it above almost every other attraction, and among the figures of their mighty dead, they revered none more highly than the prophets – those eloquent proclaimers of the truth whom heaven had sent them from age to age. Though John the Baptist did no miracles, multitudes gathered to Him because they recognized the thunder of this power in the way he spoke, which for so many generations no Jewish ear had listened to.

Jesus also was recognized as a prophet, and accordingly, His preaching created widespread excitement: *He taught in their synagogues, being glorified of all* (Luke 4:15). His words were heard with wonder and amazement. Sometimes the multitude on the shore of the lake crowded so near to Him to hear that He had to enter into a ship and speak to them from the deck as they spread themselves out in a semicircle on the ascending shore. His enemies themselves bore witness that *never man spake like this man* (John 7:46). As few as the remains are of His preaching that we possess, they are fully sufficient to make us echo the sentiment and understand the impression that He produced. All His words together that have been preserved for us would not take up more space in print than a half dozen ordinary sermons, yet it is not too much to say that they are the most precious literary heritage of the human race. His words, like His miracles, were expressions of Himself, and every one of them has in it something of the grandeur of His character.

The form of the preaching of Jesus was essentially Jewish. The Eastern mind does not work in the same way as the mind of the West. Our thinking and speaking, when at their best, are fluent, broad, and closely reasoned. The kind of speech that we admire is one that takes up an important subject, divides it into different branches, deals thoroughly with each point, shows clearly how the points relate to each other, and closes with a moving appeal to the feelings so as to sway the will to some practical result.

The mind of the East, though, loves to meditate long on a single point, to turn it around and around, to gather up all the truth around it in one focal point, and to pour it forth in a few clear and memorable words. It is concise, succinct, and wise. A Western speaker's discourse is a systematic structure, or like a chain in which link is firmly knit to link. An Oriental's is like the sky at night, full of innumerable burning points shining forth from a dark background.

This was the form of the teaching of Jesus. It consisted of numerous sayings, every one of which contained the greatest possible amount of truth in the smallest possible space, and it was expressed in language so concise and pointed as to stick in the memory like an arrow. As you read and consider them, you will find that each one of them draws the mind in and in, like a whirlpool, until it is lost in the depths. You will find, too, that there are very few of them that you do not know by heart. They have found their way into the memory of Christendom as no other words have done. Even before the meaning has been absorbed, the perfect, proverb-like expression lodges itself firmly in the mind.

There was also another characteristic of the form of Jesus' teaching. It was full of figures of speech. He taught in images. He had always been a loving and accurate observer of nature around Him, such as of the colors of the flowers, the ways of the birds, the growth of the trees, and the changes of the seasons. He was an equally skilled observer of the ways of men in all parts of life – in religion, in business, and in the home. The result was that He didn't speak without the form of some natural image.

His preaching was alive with such references, and therefore full of color, movement, and changing forms. There were no abstract statements in it, for they were all changed into pictures. Thus, in His sayings, we can still see the aspects of the country and the life of the time as in a panorama. We see the lilies, whose gorgeous beauty His eyes feasted on, waving in the fields. We see the sheep following the shepherd, the broad and narrow city gates, the young women with their lamps waiting in the darkness for the bridal procession, the Pharisee with his broad phylacteries and the publican with his bent head at prayer together in the temple, the rich man seated in his palace at a feast and the beggar lying at his gate with the dogs licking his sores, and a hundred other pictures that reveal the inner and detailed life of the time, over which history in general sweeps heedlessly with majestic stride.

The most characteristic form of speech He made use of was the parable. It was a combination of the two qualities already mentioned: the concise, memorable expression and a figurative style. It took an incident from common life and rounded into a gem-like picture in order to set forth some corresponding truth in the higher and spiritual realm.

It was a favored Jewish mode of expressing truth, but Jesus gave it by far the richest and most perfect development. About one-third of all His sayings that have been preserved to us consists of parables. This shows how they stuck in the memory. In the same way, the hearers of the sermons of any preacher will probably, after a few years, remember the sermon illustrations far better than anything else in the sermon.

These parables have remained in the memory of all generations since! The Prodigal Son (Luke 15:11-32), the Sower (Matthew 13:3-9), the Ten Virgins (Matthew 25:1-13), the Good Samaritan (Luke 10:30-37) – these and many others are pictures hung up in millions of minds. What passages in the greatest masters of expression, men such as Homer, Virgil, Dante, and

Shakespeare, have secured for themselves such a universal hold on people or have been felt to be so enduringly fresh and true?

Jesus never went far for His illustrations. As a master of painting, with a morsel of chalk or a burnt stick, will make you a face at which you must laugh, or weep, or wonder, so Jesus took the most common objects and incidents around Him – sewing a piece of cloth on an old garment, an old bottle bursting, children playing in the marketplace at weddings and funerals, or a house falling during a storm – and turned them into perfect pictures and made them instruments for conveying immortal truth to the world.

No wonder the crowds followed Him! Even the simplest people could delight in such pictures and could at least carry away as a lifelong possession the expression of His ideas, even though it might require the thought of centuries to pierce their crystal-clear depths. Never were there words so simple yet so profound, so pictorial yet so absolutely true, as the words of Jesus.

Such were the qualities of His style. The qualities of the Preacher Himself have been preserved to us in the criticisms of His hearers and are revealed in the remaining discourses that the Gospels contain.

The most prominent of His qualities in His teaching seems to have been authority: *The people were astonished at His doctrine, for He taught them as one having authority, and not as the scribes* (Mark 1:22). The first thing that stood out to His hearers was the contrast between His words and the preaching that they were used to hearing from the scribes in the synagogues. These were the defenders of the deadest and driest system of theology that has ever passed in any age for religion.

Instead of expounding the Scriptures, which were in their hands, and which would have given living power to their words, the scribes promoted the opinions of commentators, and they were afraid to support any statement unless it was backed by the authority of some master. Instead of dwelling on the great themes of justice, mercy, love, and God, they tortured the sacred text into a ceremonial manual. They preached on the proper breadth of phylacteries, the proper postures for prayer, the proper length of fasts, the distance that could be walked on the Sabbath, and so forth – for the religion of the time consisted in these things.

In order to see something in more modern times that resembles the preaching that then prevailed, we can go back to the Reformation period, when, as the historian of John Knox tells us, the lectures delivered by the monks were empty, ridiculous, and wretched in the extreme:

Legendary tales concerning the founder of some religious order, the miracles he performed, his combats with the devil, his watchings, fastings, flagellations; the virtues of holy water, chrism, crossing, and exorcism; the horrors of purgatory, and the numbers released from it by the intercessions of some powerful saint – these, with low jests, table-talk, and fireside scandal, formed the favorite topics of the preachers, and were served up to the people instead of the pure, salutary, and sublime doctrines of the Bible.[4]

The contrast that the Scottish people felt four and a half centuries ago between such lectures and the noble words of George Wishart and John Knox may convey to our mind as good an idea as can be had of the effect of the preaching of Jesus on His contemporaries. He knew nothing of the authority of masters and schools of interpretation, but He spoke as One whose own eyes had gazed on the objects of the eternal world. He did not need anyone to tell Him of God or of man, for He knew both perfectly. He was possessed with the sense of a mission that drove Him on and communicated earnestness in His every word and gesture. He knew that He had been sent from God, and the words He spoke were not His own, but God's.

---

4   This is from *The Life of John Knox*, by the Scottish historian Thomas M'Crie (1772-1835).

Jesus did not hesitate to tell those who neglected His words that in the judgment they would be condemned by the Ninevites and the Queen of Sheba, who had listened to Jonah and Solomon, for they were hearing One greater than any prophet or king of earlier times (Luke 11:29-32). He warned them that their future happiness or anguish would depend on their acceptance or rejection of the message He proclaimed. This was the tone of earnestness, majesty, and authority that struck His hearers with awe.

Another quality that the people observed in Him was boldness: *Lo, He speaketh boldly* (John 7:26). This appeared even more wonderful because He was an uneducated man who had not attended the schools of Jerusalem or received the official approval of any earthly authority. However, this quality came from the same source as His authoritativeness.

Timidity usually springs from self-consciousness. The teacher who is afraid of his audience and admires the famous and the great is thinking of himself and of what will be said of his performance. However, he who feels himself driven on by a divine mission forgets himself. All audiences are the same to him no matter who is there. He is thinking only of the message he has to deliver.

Jesus was always looking the spiritual and eternal realities in the face. The charm of their greatness held Him, and all human distinctions disappeared in their presence. People of every class were only people to Him. He was carried along on the torrent of His mission, and what might happen to Himself could not make Him stop to question or flinch.

He discovered His boldness predominantly in attacking the abuses and ideals of the time. It would be a complete mistake to think of Him as all mildness and meekness. There is hardly any aspect more conspicuous in His words than a strain of fierce indignation. It was an age of shams above almost any that have ever been. They occupied all high places. They paraded themselves in social life, occupied the chairs of learning, and above all debased every part of religion.

Hypocrisy had become so universal that it had ceased even to doubt itself. The ideals of the people were utterly low and mistaken. One can feel an indignation against all this throbbing through His words, from first to last, which had begun with His earliest observation in Nazareth and had ripened with His increasing knowledge of the times. He boldly asserted that the things that were highly esteemed among men were abomination in the sight of God (Luke 16:15). Never in the history of speech was there an argument so scathing, so annihilating, as His was against the notable characters – the scribe, the Pharisee, the priest, and the Levite – to whom the reverence of the multitude had been paid before His devastating words fell on them.

A third quality that His hearers observed was power: *His word was with power* (Luke 4:32). This was the result of that unction of the Holy One, without which even the most solemn truths fall on the ear without effect. Jesus was filled with the Spirit without measure. Therefore, the truth possessed Him. It burned and swelled in His own heart, and He proclaimed it from heart to heart. He did not just have the Spirit in such a degree as to fill Himself, but He had the Spirit in such a degree that He was able to impart the Spirit to others. The Spirit overflowed with His words and seized the souls of His hearers, filling the mind and the heart with passion.

A fourth quality that was observed in His preaching, and it was certainly a very prominent one, was graciousness: *They wondered at the gracious words which proceeded out of His mouth* (Luke 4:22). Despite His tone of authority and His fearless and scathing attacks on the times, everything Jesus said was diffused with a glow of grace and love.

His character especially spoke here. How could He who was the incarnation of love prevent the glow and warmth of the heavenly fire that dwelt in Him from spreading over His words? The scribes of the time were hard, proud, and loveless. They flattered the rich and honored the educated, but of the great majority of their hearers they said, *This people, which knoweth not the law, are cursed* (John 7:49).

To Jesus, though, every soul was infinitely precious. It did not matter what humble clothing or social deformity the pearl was hidden under. It did not even matter beneath what rubbish and filth of sin it was buried beneath. Jesus never missed it for a moment. Therefore, He spoke to His hearers of every condition and situation with the same respect. Certainly it was the divine love itself, uttering itself from the innermost depth of the divine being, that spoke in the parables of Luke 15.

These were some of the qualities of the Preacher. One more can be mentioned, and this one can be said to embrace all the rest. It is possibly the highest quality of public speech. Jesus addressed people as people, and not as members of any class or possessors of any specific culture. The differences that divide people, such as wealth, power, and education, are on the surface. The qualities in which they are all alike – the broad sense of the understanding, the great passions of the heart, and the primary instincts of the conscience – are profound.

These are not the same in all people, of course. In some they are deeper, and in others they are shallower, but in all people they are far deeper than anything else. He who addresses them appeals to the deepest part in his hearers. He will be equally understandable to all. Every hearer will receive his own portion from Him. The small and shallow mind will get as much as it can take, and the largest and deepest will get its fill at the same feast. This is why the words of Jesus are perennial in their freshness. They are for all generations, and they are equally for all. They appeal to the deepest elements in human nature today in America or England or China as much as they did in Israel when they were spoken.

When we come to inquire what topics the preaching of Jesus

consisted of, we might naturally expect to find Him expounding the system of doctrine that we ourselves are acquainted with, in the forms of something like a catechism or a confession of faith. However, what we find is very different.

Jesus did not make use of any system of doctrine. We can hardly doubt that all the many and different ideas of His preaching, as well as those that He never expressed, existed in His mind together as one body of rounded truth – but that is not how they existed in His teaching. He did not use theological terms. He did not speak of the Trinity, of predestination, or of effectual calling, although His words support the ideas that these terms convey, and it is the undoubted task of science to bring them forth. Instead, Jesus spoke in the language of life, and He concentrated His preaching on a few burning points that touched the heart, the conscience, and the time.

The central idea and the most common phrase of His preaching was *the kingdom of God* (e.g., Matthew 6:33; 12:28; 19:24; and 21:43). Many of His parables begin with *The kingdom of heaven is like . . .* (e.g., Matthew 13:31-52; 20:1-2). Jesus said, *I must preach the kingdom of God to other cities also* (Luke 4:43), thereby characterizing the matter of His preaching. In the same way, He sent forth the apostles *to preach the kingdom of God* (Luke 9:2). He did not invent the phrase. It was a historical one handed down from the past and was common in the mouths of His contemporaries. John the Baptist had made much use of it, the central theme of his message being, *The kingdom of God is at hand* (Mark 1:15).

What did it signify? It signified the new era that the prophets had predicted and the saints had looked for. Jesus announced that it had come and that He had brought it. The time of waiting was fulfilled. Many prophets and righteous men, He told His contemporaries, had desired to see the things that they saw, but had not seen them (Matthew 13:17; Luke 10:24). He declared that the privileges and glories of the new time were so great that the least partaker of them was greater than John the Baptist, even though he had been the greatest representative of the old time (Matthew 11:11).

This was what His contemporaries would have expected to hear if they had recognized that the kingdom of God was really come, but they looked around and asked where the new era was that Jesus said He had brought. This is where He and they were at complete variance. They emphasized the first part of the phrase, *the kingdom*, while He emphasized the second, *of God*. They expected the new era to appear in magnificent physical forms – in a kingdom of which God indeed was to be the ruler, but which was to show itself in worldly splendor, in force of arms, and as a universal empire. Jesus saw the new era as an empire of God over the loving heart and the obedient will. They looked for it outside. Jesus said, *The kingdom of God is within you* (Luke 17:21).

They looked for a period of external glory and happiness, while Jesus placed the glory and blessedness of the new time in character. That is why He began His Sermon on the Mount, that great manifesto of the new era, with a series of "Blesseds" (Matthew 5:1-12). The blessedness, though, was entirely that of character, and it was a character totally different from that which was then looked up to as imparting glory and happiness to its possessor – that of the proud Pharisee, the wealthy Sadducee, or the educated scribe. Blessed, said He, are the poor in spirit, those who mourn, the meek, those who hunger and thirst after righteousness, the merciful, the pure in heart, the peacemakers, and those who are persecuted for righteousness' sake.

The main gist of His preaching was to set forth this understanding of the kingdom of God, the character of its members, their blessedness in the love and communion of their Father in heaven, and their prospects in the glory of the future world. Jesus showed the contrast between it and the formal religion of the time, with its lack of spirituality and its substitution of ceremonial observances for character.

Jesus invited all groups of people into the kingdom. He invited the rich, as in the parable of the Rich Man and Lazarus, by showing the emptiness and danger of seeking their blessedness in wealth. He invited the poor by impressing upon them the sense of their dignity, persuading them with the most overflowing affection and winning words that the only true wealth was in character, assuring them that if they sought first the kingdom of God, their heavenly Father, who fed the ravens and clothed the lilies, would not allow them to be in need (Matthew 6:25-34).

The center and soul of His preaching, though, was Himself. He contained within Himself the new era. He not only announced it, but He created it. The new character that made people subjects of the kingdom and sharers of its privileges was to be obtained from Him alone. Therefore, the practical issue of every discourse of Christ was the command to come to Him, to learn of Him, and to follow Him. *Come unto me, all ye that labor and are heavy laden* was the keynote, the deepest and final word of all His discourses (Matthew 11:28).

It is impossible to read the discourses of Jesus without noticing that as wonderful as they are, some of the most characteristic doctrines of Christianity, as set forth in the epistles of Paul and now cherished in the minds of the most devoted and enlightened Christians, hold a very inconsiderable place in them. This is especially the case in regard to the great doctrines of the gospel as to how a sinner is reconciled to God, and how, in a pardoned soul, the character is gradually produced that makes it like Christ and pleasing to the Father.

The lack of reference to such doctrines may indeed be much exaggerated since there is not one prominent doctrine of the great apostle in which the beginnings are not to be found in the teaching of Christ Himself. Yet the contrast is distinct enough to have given some pretense for denying that the distinctive doctrines of Paul are genuine elements of Christianity. The true explanation of the phenomenon, though, is very different.

Jesus was not a mere teacher. His character was greater than His words, as was His work. The main part of that work was to atone for the sins of the world by His death on the cross. His closest followers never really believed that He was to die, though, and until His death occurred, it was impossible to explain its far-reaching significance. Paul's most distinctive doctrines are merely expositions of the meaning of two great facts: the death of Christ and the mission of the Spirit by the glorified Redeemer. It is obvious that these facts could not be fully explained in the words of Jesus Himself when they had not yet taken place, but to suppress the inspired explanation of them would be to extinguish the light of the gospel and rob Christ of His crowning glory.

The audience of Jesus varied greatly both in size and character on different occasions. Very frequently it was a great multitude. He addressed them everywhere – on the mountain, on the seashore, on the highway, in the synagogues, and in the temple courts. He was also quite willing to speak with a single individual, however lowly. He took advantage of every opportunity of doing so. Although He was worn out with fatigue, He talked to the woman at the well (John 4:6-42). He received Nicodemus alone (John 3:1-21). He taught Mary in her home (Luke 10:38-42).

There are about nineteen such private conversations mentioned in the Gospels. They leave a memorable example to His followers. This is probably the most effective of all forms of instruction, as it is certainly the best test of earnestness. A man who preaches to thousands with enthusiasm might be a mere orator, but the person who seeks the opportunity of speaking closely to individuals of the welfare of their souls must have a real fire from heaven burning in his heart.

His audience often consisted of the circle of His disciples.

His preaching divided His hearers. He includes Himself in such parables as the Sower (Matthew 13:3-9), the Tares and the Wheat (Matthew 13:24-30, 36-43), and the Wedding Feast (Matthew 22:1-14), which described its effects on different classes with unequalled vividness.

Jesus' teaching utterly repelled some people. Others heard it with wonder without being touched in the heart. Others were affected for a time, but soon returned to their old interests. It is awful to think how few there were, even when the Son of God was preaching, who heard unto salvation. Those who did so gradually formed around Him a body of disciples. They followed Him around, hearing all His discourses, and He often spoke to them alone.

Such were the five hundred to whom He appeared in Galilee after His resurrection (1 Corinthians 15:6). Some of them were women, such as Mary Magdalene, Susanna, and Joanna, the wife of Herod's steward, who, being wealthy, gladly supplied His few simple needs. To these disciples He gave a more thorough instruction than to the crowd. He explained to them in private whatever they did not understand in His public teaching.

More than once He made the statement that He spoke in parables to the multitudes so that, though hearing, they might not understand (Matthew 13:10-17). This could only mean that those who had no real interest in the truth were sent away with the mere beautiful shell, but no understanding.

To those who had a spiritual thirst for more, Jesus gladly communicated the hidden secret. When the nation as a whole declared itself unworthy of being the channel of the Messiah's worldwide influence, these disciples became the nucleus of that spiritual society, elevated above all local limitations and distinctions of rank and nationality, in which the spirit and doctrine of Christ were to be spread and perpetuated throughout the world.

The Apostles

Perhaps the formation of the group known as the apostles should be placed side by side with miracles and preaching as a third means by which Jesus did His work. The men who became the twelve apostles were at first only ordinary disciples like many others. This, at least, was the position of those who were already His followers during the first year of His ministry. At the opening of His Galilean activity, their attachment to Him entered on a second stage when He called them to give up their ordinary employments and be with Him constantly. It was probably not many weeks later that He promoted them to the third and final stage of nearness to Himself by ordaining them to be apostles (Luke 6:13).

When His work grew so extensive and demanding that it was quite impossible for Him to keep up with it all, He multiplied Himself, so to speak, by appointing His disciples to be His assistants. He commissioned them to teach the simpler elements of His doctrine and conferred on them miraculous powers similar to His own (Matthew 10:5-15). In this way, many towns were evangelized that He did not have time to visit, and many people were cured who could not have been brought into contact with Him.

However, as future events proved, His purposes in appointing them were much more far-reaching. His work was for all time and for the whole world. It could not be accomplished in a single lifetime. He foresaw this and made provision for it by the early choice of representatives who could take up His plans after He was gone, and in whom He could still extend His influence over mankind. He did not write any of the Scriptures Himself. We might think that writing would have been the best way of perpetuating His influence and giving the world a perfect image of Himself, and we cannot help imagining with a glimmer of strong desire what a volume penned by His hand would have been. However, for wise reasons He abstained from this kind of work and resolved to live after death in the lives of chosen men and women.

It is surprising to see what sort of people Jesus selected for such an important role. They did not belong to the influential and educated classes. No doubt the heads and leaders of the nation should have been the mouthpieces of their Messiah, but they proved themselves totally unworthy of the great vocation. He was able to do without them. He did not need the influence of worldly power and wisdom.

Always wanting to work with the elements of character that are not limited to any station of life or class of culture, He did not hesitate to commit His cause to twelve men, most of whom lacked learning and belonged to the common people. He made the selection after a night spent in prayer (Luke 6:12). The event showed with what insight into God's will He had acted.

The disciples turned out to be instruments entirely qualified for the great plan. Two at least, John and Peter, were men of supreme gifts, and one of the disciples was a traitor. The choice of Judas will probably, even after all explanations, always remain a very partially explained mystery, yet the selection of ambassadors who were at first so unlikely, but in the end proved so successful, will always be one of the finest monuments of the incomparable originality of Jesus.

It would, however, be a very inadequate account of His relation to the Twelve merely to point out the insight with which He discerned in them their potential for their grand future. They became very great men, and in the founding of the Christian church achieved a work of immeasurable importance. In a sense they little dreamed of, they could be said to sit on thrones ruling the modern world (Matthew 19:28). They stand like a row of noble pillars towering far across the plains of time. The sunlight that shines on them and makes them visible, though, comes entirely from Him.

Jesus gave them all their greatness, and their greatness is one of the most remarkable evidences of His greatness. What must He have been, whose influence imparted to them such magnitude of character and made them ready for such a gigantic task! At first, they were rude and earthly in the extreme. What hope was there that they would ever be able to appreciate the intentions of a mind like His, to inherit His work, to possess in any degree a spirit so admirable, and to transmit to future generations a faithful image of His character?

However, He educated them with the most affectionate patience, bearing with their unrefined hopes and their clumsy misunderstandings of His meaning. Never forgetting for a moment the part they were to play in the future, He made their training His most constant work. They were much more constantly in His company than even the general body of His disciples, seeing all He did in public and hearing all He said. They were often His only audience, and then He unveiled to them the glories and mysteries of His doctrine, sowing in their minds the seeds of truth that time and experience were to cause to bear fruit in time.

The most important part of their training, though, was one that might not have been noticed much at the time, although it was producing splendid results: the silent and constant influence of His character on theirs. He drew them to Himself and stamped His own image on them. It was this that made them the men they became. For this, more than anything else, the generations of those who love Jesus look back to them with envy. We admire and adore at a distance the qualities of His character, but what must it have been to see them in the unity of life, and for years to feel their shaping and influencing strength! Can we recall with any fullness the features of this character whose glory they beheld and under whose power they lived?

The Human Character of Jesus

The most obvious feature that they would notice in Jesus might have been purposefulness. This certainly is the common note that resounds in all His sayings that have been preserved for us, and it is the pulse that we feel beating in all His recorded actions. He was possessed with a purpose that guided Him and drove Him on.

Most lives aim at nothing in particular, but simply drift along under the influence of varying moods and instincts or on the currents of society and achieve nothing. But Jesus evidently had a definite object before Him that absorbed His thoughts and drew out His energies. He would often give as a reason for not doing something, *Mine hour is not yet come* (John 2:4), as if His purpose absorbed every moment, and every hour had its own appointed part of the task.

This gave an earnestness and swiftness of execution to His life that most lives generally lack. It saved Him, too, from spending energy on details and being meticulous about little things on which those who do not follow any definite call give themselves to completely. This made His life, as various as its activities were, an unbroken unity.

Very closely connected with this quality was another prominent one that can be called faith. By this we mean His astonishing confidence in the accomplishment of His purpose and His apparent disregard both of assets and opposition. If it is considered in the most general way how massive His purpose was – to reform His nation and begin an everlasting and worldwide religious movement – if the opposition that He encountered and foresaw that His cause would have to meet at every stage of its progress is considered, and if it is remembered that as a man He was an uneducated Galilean peasant, then His quiet and unwavering confidence in His success will appear only less remarkable than His success itself.

After reading the Gospels through, one asks in wonder what Jesus did to produce such a mighty impression on the world. He did not construct any elaborate system to ensure the effect. He did not lay hold of the centers of influence, such as learning, wealth, and government. It is true that He instituted the church, but He left no detailed explanations of its nature or rules for how it was to be managed.

This was the simplicity of faith that does not contrive and prepare, but simply goes onward and does the work. It was the quality that He said could remove mountains and that He especially desired in His followers (Matthew 21:21). This was the foolishness of the gospel of which Paul boasted as it was going forth in the resoluteness of power, but with laughable meagerness of devices and resources to overcome the Greek and Roman world (1 Corinthians 1:17-25).

A third prominent feature of the character of Jesus was originality. Most lives are easily explained. They are mere products of circumstances, and there are thousands of copies like them that surround them or have preceded them. We are each formed by the habits and customs of the country to which we belong, the fashion and tastes of our generation, the traditions of our education, the prejudices of our class, and the opinions of our school or sect. We do work determined for us by an incidental collection of circumstances. Our convictions are ingrained on us by authority from without instead of growing naturally from within. Our opinions are blown to us in fragments on every wind.

What circumstances formed and made the Man Christ Jesus, though? There was never an age more dry and barren than that in which He was born. He was like a tall, fresh palm tree springing out of a desert. What was there in the petty life of Nazareth to produce such a gigantic character? How could the notoriously wicked village send forth such breathing purity?

Maybe a scribe taught Him the alphabet and grammar,

but His doctrine was a complete contradiction of all that the scribes taught. The trends of the sects never laid hold of His free spirit. How clearly, amid the sounds that filled the ears of His time, He heard the neglected voice of truth, which was quite different from the religious leaders! How clearly, behind all the pretentious and accepted forms of religion, He saw the lovely and neglected figure of real godliness!

He cannot be explained by anything that was in the world that could have shaped Him. He grew from within. Instead of allowing His vision to be informed by what others had said they saw, He directed His eyes straight to the facts of nature and life and believed what He Himself saw. He was equally loyal to the truth in His words. He went forth and proclaimed what He believed without hesitation, although it shook the institutions, the creeds, and customs of His country to their foundations, and it loosened the opinions of the common people in a hundred points in which they had been educated.

It may indeed be said that although the Jewish nation of Jesus' own time was an utterly dry ground out of which no green and great thing could be expected to grow, He reverted to the earlier history of His nation and nourished His mind on the ideas of Moses and the prophets. There is some truth in this, but affectionate and constant as His familiarity with them was, He handled them with a free and fearless hand. He redeemed them from themselves and demonstrated in maturity the ideas that they taught only in seed form.

What a contrast between the covenant God of Israel and the Father in heaven whom He revealed! What a difference between the temple, with its priests and bloody sacrifices, and the worship in spirit and in truth! What a difference between the national and ceremonial morality of the Law and the morality of the conscience and the heart! Even in comparison with the figures of Moses, Elijah, and Isaiah, Jesus towers over others in originality.

A fourth and very glorious feature of His character was His love for His Father and for people. It has already been said that He was consumed with an overmastering purpose. There must be a great passion beneath a great life purpose that shapes and sustains it. Love for God and others was the passion that directed and inspired Jesus.

We have not been informed with any detail how the love for individuals sprang up and grew in the seclusion of Nazareth and on what materials it fed. We only know that when Jesus appeared in public, it was a leading passion that completely swallowed up self-love, filled Him with limitless compassion for human despair, and enabled Him to go forward without once looking back in the business to which He devoted Himself.

We know only in general that it drew its support from the understanding He had of the infinite value of the human soul. It surpassed all the limits that other people have to put to their compassion. Differences of class and nationality usually moderate people's interest in each other. In nearly all countries, it has been considered a virtue to hate one's enemies. It is generally agreed to despise and avoid those who have defiled the laws of respectability.

However, Jesus paid no attention to these practices. The overpowering sense of the preciousness that He perceived in enemy, foreigner, and outcast alike prevented Him from doing so. This marvelous love shaped the purpose of His life. It gave Him the most tender and intense empathy with every form of pain and misery. It was His deepest reason for healing others. His merciful heart drew Him wherever help was most needed.

His love especially induced Him to save the soul. He knew this was the real jewel. He understood that everything should be done to rescue the soul and that its miseries and perils were the most dangerous of all. Some people have loved others without this fundamental purpose, but the love of Jesus was directed by wisdom to the truest happiness of those He loved.

He knew He was doing His very best for them when He was saving them from their sins.

The crowning attribute of Jesus' human character was love to God. It is the greatest honor and achievement of man to be one with God in feeling, thought, and purpose. Jesus had this in perfection. It is very difficult for us to realize God. The great majority of people hardly think about Him at all, and even the godliest confess that it takes much effort to discipline their minds into the habit of constantly realizing Him.

When we do think of Him, it is with a painful sense of a disharmony between what is in us and what is in Him. We cannot remain, even for a few minutes, in His presence without the sense, in greater or less degree, that His thoughts are not our thoughts, nor are His ways our ways (Isaiah 55:8-9).

It was not this way with Jesus. He always realized God. He never spent an hour and never did anything without direct reference to God. God was around Him like the air He breathed or the sunlight in which He walked. His thoughts were God's thoughts. His desires were never in the least different from God's. His purpose, He was perfectly sure, was God's purpose for Him.

How did He attain this absolute harmony with God? To a large extent, it must be attributed to the perfect harmony of His nature within itself, yet in some measure He got it by the same means by which we laboriously seek it: by studying God's thoughts and purposes in His Word, which from His childhood was His constant delight; by cultivating the habit of prayer His entire life, for which He found time even when He did not have time to eat; and by patiently resisting temptations to entertain thoughts and purposes of His own that were different from God's.

These are the things that gave Him such faith and fearlessness in His work. He knew that the call to do it had come from God, and He knew that He was immortal until it was done.

This was what made Him, with all His self-consciousness and originality, the pattern of meekness and submission, for He was forever bringing every thought and wish into obedience to His Father's will.

This was the secret of the peace and majestic calmness that imparted such a stateliness to His demeanor in the most difficult hours of life. He knew that the worst that could happen to Him was His Father's will for Him, and that was enough. He always had near Him a retreat of perfect rest, silence, and sunshine into which He could find refuge from the clamor and confusion around Him. This was the great secret He passed on to His followers when He said to them at His departure, *Peace I leave with you; My peace I give unto you* (John 14:27).

The sinlessness of Jesus has been often discussed as the crowning attribute of His character. The Scriptures, which so clearly record the sins of their very greatest heroes, such as Abraham and Moses, have no sins of His to record. There is no more prominent characteristic of the saints of antiquity than their repentance. The more eminently saintly they were, the more abundant and bitter were their tears and lamentations over their sinfulness. However, although it is acknowledged by all that Jesus was the supreme religious figure of history, He never demonstrated this characteristic of saintliness; He confessed no sin.

Is this not because He had no sin to confess? Yet the idea of sinlessness is too negative to express the perfection of His character. He was sinless, but He was sinless because He was completely full of love.

Sin against God is merely the expression of lack of love to God, and sin against man is simply because of lack of love to man. Someone full of love to both God and man cannot possibly sin against either. This fullness of love to His Father and His fellow men, governing every aspect of His being, constituted the perfection of His character.

The twelve apostles owed all they became to the impression produced on them by their long-continued contact with their Master. We cannot determine with certainty at what precise time they began to realize the central truth of the Christianity they were later to publish to the world – that behind the tenderness and majesty of this human character there was in Jesus something still more noble – or by what stages their impressions matured to the full conviction that in Christ Jesus perfect manhood was in union with perfect Deity.

This was the goal of all the revelations of Himself that He made to them, but the breakdown of their faith at His death shows how immature up until that time their convictions must have been in regard to His personality, however worthily they were able, in certain pleasant hours, to express their faith in Him. It was the experience of the resurrection and ascension that gave to the shifting impressions, which had long been accumulating in their minds, the touch by which they were made to solidify into the immovable conviction that in Him with whom it had been granted to them to associate so intimately, God was manifest in the flesh.

Chapter 6

The Year of Opposition

For an entire year, Jesus pursued His work in Galilee with incessant energy, moving among the poor crowds that sought His miraculous help, seizing every opportunity of pouring His words of grace and truth into the ears of the multitude or of the solitary concerned inquirer. In hundreds of homes to whose residents He had restored health and joy, His name must have become a household word. In thousands of minds whose depths His preaching had stirred, He must have been cherished with gratitude and love.

Wider and wider rang the echoes of His fame. For a time, it seemed as if everyone in Galilee would become one of His disciples, and as if the growing movement would easily roll southward, overwhelming all opposition and covering the entire land in an enthusiasm of love for the Healer and of obedience to the Teacher.

The twelve months had scarcely passed, though, when it became sadly evident that this was not to be. The Galilean mind turned out to be stony ground, where the seed of the kingdom quickly sprouted up, but just as quickly withered away. The change was sudden and complete, and it at once changed all the features of the life of Jesus.

He remained in Galilee for six more months, but these months were very different from the first twelve. The voices that rose around Him were no longer the ringing shouts of gratitude and applause, but voices of opposition, bitter and blasphemous. He was no longer to be seen moving from one crowded place to another in the heart of the country, welcomed everywhere by those who waited to experience or to see His miracles, and followed by thousands of people who were eager to hear every word of His discourses.

Jesus was a fugitive, seeking the most distant and remote places, accompanied only by a handful of followers. At the end of the six months, He left Galilee forever, but He did not leave as one might have previously thought He would have left. He was not carried aloft on the wave of public acknowledgment to make an easy conquest of the hearts of the people in the southern part of the country, taking victorious possession of a Jerusalem unable to resist the unanimous voice of the people.

He did indeed labor for six more months in the southern part of the land, in Judea and Perea, and where His miracles were seen for the first time, there were still the same signs of public enthusiasm that had greeted Him in the first months of joy in Galilee – but the most that He accomplished was to add a few people to the company of His faithful disciples. From the day He left Galilee, He did indeed set His face steadfastly toward Jerusalem, and the six months He spent in Perea and Judea can be regarded as occupied with a slow journey there.

However, the journey was begun in the full assurance, which He openly expressed to the disciples, that in the capital He was to receive no triumph over enthusiastic hearts and convinced minds, but would meet with a definite national rejection and would be killed instead of crowned. We must trace the causes and the progress of this change in the sentiment of the Galileans and in this sad turn in the career of Jesus.

From the very beginning, the educated and influential classes had taken up an attitude of opposition to Him. The more worldly sections of them – the Sadducees and Herodians – did not pay much attention to Him at first. They had their own business to take care of – their wealth, their court influence, and their amusements. They did not care much about a religious movement going on among the lower class of people. The public rumor that someone professing to be the Messiah had appeared did not excite their interest, for they did not share the popular expectations on the subject. They said to one another that this was just one more pretender whom the strange ideas of the general public were sure to raise up from time to time. It was only when the movement seemed to them to be threatening to lead to a political revolt that would bring down the iron hand of the Roman masters on the country, provide the procurator an excuse for new extortions, and endanger their property and comforts that they began to pay any attention to Him.

It was very different, however, with the more religious sections of the upper class – the Pharisees and scribes. They took the deepest interest in all ecclesiastical and religious developments. A movement of a religious kind among the people excited their eager attention, for they themselves desired popular influence. A new voice with the ring of prophecy in it, or the proclamation of any new doctrine or belief, caught their ear at once. More than anything else, anyone putting himself forward as the Messiah produced the utmost excitement among them, for they passionately cherished messianic hopes and were at the time severely hurting under the foreign domination.

In relation to the rest of the community, they were similar to our clergy and leading religious laymen, and probably formed about the same proportion of the population and exercised at least as great an influence as these do among us. It has been estimated that they may have numbered about six thousand. They were thought of as the best people in the country, the caretakers of respectability and religion. The people looked up to them as those who had the right to judge and determine in all religious matters.

They cannot be accused of having neglected Jesus. They turned their earnest attention to Him from the beginning. They followed Him step by step. They discussed His doctrines and His claims and made up their minds. Their decision was unfavorable to the cause of Christ, and they followed it up with action, never slacking in their activity for even an hour.

Perhaps the most solemn and appalling circumstance in the whole tragedy of the life of Christ was that the men who rejected, hunted down, and murdered Him were those regarded as the best in the nation, its teachers and examples, the zealous protectors of the Bible and the traditions of the past. These men, who were eagerly waiting for the Messiah, judged Jesus, as they believed, according to the Scriptures, and thought they were obeying the dictates of conscience and doing God service when they treated Him as they did.

There cannot fail sometimes to sweep across the mind of a reader of the Gospels a strong feeling of pity for them and a kind of sympathy with them. Jesus was so unlike the Messiah whom they were looking for and whom their fathers had taught them to expect! He so completely counteracted their prejudices and beliefs, and He dishonored so many things that they had been taught to regard as sacred! They can certainly be pitied. There was never a crime like their crime, and there was never a punishment like their punishment.

There is the same sadness about the fate of those who are thrown upon any great crisis of the world's history and, not understanding the signs of the times, make fatal mistakes, just as they did, for example, who at the Reformation were unable to go forth and join the movement of God.

What was their basic situation? It was that they were so blinded with sin that they could not recognize the light. Their views of the Messiah had been distorted by centuries of worldliness and lack of godliness of which they were the like-minded heirs. They thought Jesus was a sinner because He did not conform to ordinances that they and their fathers had irreverently added to those of God's Word, and because their concept of a good man, which He did not fit, was completely false. Jesus supplied them with enough evidence of who He was, but they didn't have eyes to see it.

There is something at the bottom of honest and true hearts that, no matter how long and deeply it may have been buried under prejudice and sin, leaps up with joy and a desire to embrace what is true, what is holy, and what is pure and great when it draws near. But nothing of the kind was found in these people. Their hearts were withered, hardened, and dead. They brought their established rules and arbitrary standards to judge Him by, and they were never shaken by His greatness from the fatal attitude of denunciation.

He brought truth near them, but they did not have the truth-loving ear to recognize the sound. He brought the whitest purity near them, such purity that archangels would have veiled their faces at, but they were not affected. He brought near them the very face of mercy and heavenly love, but their dim eyes made no response. We may, indeed, pity the conduct of such people as a sad misfortune, but it is better to fear and tremble at it as astounding sin.

The more utterly wicked people become, the more inevitable it is that they will sin. The more immense the accumulation of a nation's sin becomes as it rolls down through the centuries, the more inevitable does some terrible national transgression become. When the inevitable takes place, it is not an object for pity only, but also for holy and jealous wrath.

One thing about Jesus that stirred up their opposition to Him from the beginning was the humbleness of His origin. They were impressed with the ordinary bias toward the rich and the educated, and they could not recognize the nobility of the soul apart from the circumstances of position and culture. Jesus was a son of the people. He had been a carpenter. They believed He had been born in coarse and wicked Galilee. He had not passed through the schools of Jerusalem, and He had not drunk from the acknowledged wells of wisdom there. They thought that a prophet, and above all the Messiah, would have been born in Judea, reared at Jerusalem in the center of culture and religion, and allied with all that was distinguished and influential in the nation.

For the same reason, they were offended with the followers He chose and the company He kept. His chosen disciples were not selected from among themselves, the wise and highborn, but were uneducated laymen and poor fishermen. One of them was even a publican, a tax collector. Probably nothing that Jesus did gave greater offense than the choice of Matthew, the tax collector, to be an apostle. The tax collectors, as servants of the foreign power, were hated for their trade, their extortions, and their character by all who were patriotic and respectable. How could Jesus hope that respectable and educated men would enter a circle such as that which He had formed around Himself? Besides, He mingled freely with the lowest class of the population – with tax collectors, prostitutes, and other sinners.

In Christian times, we have learned to love Jesus for this more than anything else. We easily see that if He really was the Savior from sin, He could not have been found in more appropriate company than among those who needed salvation most. We know now how He could believe that many of the lost were more the victims of circumstances than sinners by choice, and that if He drew the magnet across the top of the rubbish, it would attract to itself many pieces of precious metal.

The purest-minded and highest-born people have since learned to follow His footsteps down into the regions of filth and sin to seek and save the lost, but until Jesus came, that idea was largely foreign to humanity. The majority of sinners outside the limits of respectability were despised and hated as the enemies of society, and no efforts were made to save them. On the contrary, all who aimed at religious distinction avoided their very touch as defilement.

Simon the Pharisee, when he was entertaining Jesus, never doubted that if Jesus had been a prophet and had known who the woman was who was touching Him, He would have driven her away (Luke 7:36-50). That was the sentiment of the time. Yet when Jesus brought the new sentiment into the world and showed them the divine face of mercy, they should have recognized it. If their hearts had not been completely hard and cruel, they would have jumped up to welcome this revelation of a more heavenly humanity. The light of sinners forsaking their evil ways, of wicked women sobbing for their lost lives, and of extortioners like Zacchaeus becoming sincere and generous should have delighted them – but it did not, and they only hated Jesus for His compassion, calling Him a friend of publicans and sinners (Matthew 11:19).

A third and very serious reason for their opposition was that He did not Himself practice, nor encourage His disciples to practice, many ritual observances, such as ceremonial washing of the hands before meals, and so forth, which were then considered the marks of a saintly man. It has been already explained how these practices arose. They had been invented in an earnest but mechanical age in order to emphasize the distinctiveness of Jewish character and to keep up the separation of the Jews from other nations.

The original intention was good, but the end result was deplorable. It was soon forgotten that they were merely human inventions. They were supposed to be binding by divine sanction, but God did not approve of these human inventions. They increased until they regulated every hour of the day and every action of life. They were made the substitutes for real piety and morality by the majority. They were an intolerable burden to tender consciences, for it was hardly possible to move a step or lift a finger without the danger of sinning against one or another of them.

However, no one doubted their authority, and the careful observance of them was reputed to be the badge of a godly life. Jesus regarded them as the great evil of the time. He therefore neglected them and encouraged others to do so – not, however, without at the same time leading the people back to the great principles of judgment, mercy, and faith (Matthew 23:23), and making them feel the majesty of the conscience and the depth and spirituality of the law. The result was that He was looked upon as an ungodly man and a deceiver of the people.

It was especially in regard to the Sabbath that this difference between Him and the religious teachers came out. Their inventions of restrictions and arbitrary rules in this area had run into the most pompous extravagance until they had changed the day of rest, joy, and blessing into an intolerable burden.

Jesus was in the habit of performing His cures on the Sabbath. They thought such work was a breach of the command. Jesus exposed the wrongness of their objections again and again by explaining the nature of the institution itself as *made for man* (Mark 2:27), by reference to the practice of ancient saints (Matthew 12:3-5), and even by the analogy of some of their own practices on the holy day (Matthew 12:11). However, they were not convinced, and since He continued His practice in spite of their objections, this remained a continued and bitter reason for their hatred.

Since they arrived at these conclusions on such improper reasoning, it will be easily understood that they were utterly unwilling to listen to Him when He put forward His higher claims – when He announced Himself as the Messiah, professed to forgive sins, and provided indications of His high relation to God. Having concluded that He was an impostor and deceiver, they regarded such assertions as hideous blasphemies, and they could not help wanting to stop the mouth that uttered them.

It might cause surprise that they were not convinced by His miracles. If Jesus really performed the numerous and amazing miracles that are recorded of Him, how could they resist such evidence of His divine mission? The debate that was held with the authorities by the tough reasoner whom Jesus cured of blindness, and whose case is recorded in the ninth chapter of John, shows how severely they might sometimes have been pressured with such reasoning. However, they had satisfied themselves with a defiant reply to it.

It is to be remembered that among the Jews, miracles had never been looked upon as conclusive proof of a divine mission. They could have been worked by false as well as true prophets. They could be traceable to diabolical instead of divine power. Whether they were so or not was to be determined by other factors. Based upon these factors, they had concluded that Jesus had not been sent from God, so they attributed His miracles to an alliance with the powers of darkness. Jesus met this blasphemous conclusion with the utmost force of holy indignation and conclusive argument, but it is easy to see that it was a position in which minds like those of His opponents might entrench themselves with a sense of much security (Matthew 12:24-28).

They had formed their adverse judgment of Him very early, and they never changed it. Even during His first year in Judea, they had pretty well decided against Him. When the news of His success in Galilee spread, they were filled with dismay, and they sent representatives from Jerusalem to work in agreement with their local adherents in opposing Him. Even during His year of joy, He clashed with them again and again.

At first, Jesus treated them with consideration and appealed to their reason and heart. Soon, though, He saw that this was hopeless, and He accepted their opposition as inevitable. He exposed the hollowness of their pretensions to His audiences and warned His disciples against them. Meanwhile, they did everything to poison the public mind against Him. They succeeded only too well. When the tide of His popularity began to recede at the end of the year, they pressed their advantage, assailing Him more and more boldly.

They even soon succeeded in arousing the cold minds of the Sadducees and Herodians against Him, no doubt by persuading them that He was promoting a popular revolt that would endanger the throne of their master Herod, who reigned over Galilee. That mean and characterless ruler himself also became His persecutor. Herod had other reasons to fear Him besides those suggested by his attendants.

About this very time, Herod had murdered John the Baptist. It was one of the lowest and most corrupt crimes recorded in history. It was a dreadful example of the way in which sin leads to sin, and of the malicious perseverance that a wicked woman will embrace to enact her revenge. Soon after it was committed, Herod's attendants went to tell him of the supposed political plans of Jesus. When he heard of the new prophet, an awful thought went through his guilty conscience: *It is John the Baptist*, he said, *whom I beheaded; he is risen from the dead* (Mark 6:16).

Still, Herod wanted to see Jesus, his curiosity getting the better of his fear (Luke 9:9). It was the desire of the lion to see the lamb. Jesus never responded to Herod's invitation, and it just might have been because of this that Herod was even more willing to listen to the suggestion of his attendants that he should arrest Him as a dangerous person. Soon after this, Herod was seeking to kill Jesus (Luke 13:31). Jesus had to keep out of Herod's way, and no doubt this helped, along with more important things, to change the character of His life in Galilee during the last six months of His stay there.

It had seemed for a time as if His hold on the mind and the heart of the common people might become so strong as to result in an irresistible national acceptance. Many movements, frowned upon at first by authorities and dignitaries, have risen to take possession of the upper classes and carry the centers of influence by committing themselves to the lower classes and securing their enthusiastic acknowledgment. There is a certain point of national consent at which any movement that reaches it becomes like a flood that no amount of animosity or official enmity can successfully oppose.

Jesus gave Himself to the common people of Galilee, and in return they gave Him their love and admiration. Instead of hating Him like the Pharisees and scribes, and calling Him a glutton and a winebibber (Matthew 11:19), they believed that he was a prophet. They compared Him to the very greatest figures of the past, and many, as they were more struck with the heavenly or with the tender side of His teaching, said He was Isaiah or Jeremiah risen from the dead (Matthew 16:13-14).

It was a common idea of the time that the coming of the Messiah was to be preceded by the rising again of some prophet. The prophet most commonly considered was Elijah. Accordingly, some took Jesus for Elijah. However, they only thought that he was a forerunner of the Messiah, not the actual Messiah. He was not at all like their idea of the coming Deliverer, which was of the most absolute physical kind. Indeed, every once in a while after He had performed some unusually remarkable miracle, there might be raised a single voice or a few voices suggesting that Jesus might be the Messiah. However, as wonderful as His deeds and His words were, the entire aspect of His life was so unlike their preconceptions that the truth failed to suggest itself forcibly and universally to their minds.

At last, however, the decisive hour seemed to have arrived. That great turning point has already been alluded to – the end of the twelve months in Galilee. Jesus had heard of John the Baptist's death, and He immediately went away into a desert place with His disciples to grieve and talk over the tragic event.

He sailed to the eastern side of the lake, and landing on the grassy plain of Bethsaida, went up to a hill with the Twelve.

Soon, though, an immense multitude gathered at the foot of the hill to hear and see Him. They had found out where He was, and they gathered to Him from all around. Always ready to sacrifice Himself for others, Jesus descended to address and heal them. He continued to speak as the evening arrived. Then, moved with much compassion for the helpless multitude, He performed the wonderful miracle of feeding the five thousand (Mark 6:35-46). Its effect was overwhelming. The people became immediately convinced that this was none other than the Messiah, and having only one idea of what this meant, they attempted to take Him by force and make Him a king (John 6:14-15). That is, they tried to force Him to become the leader of a messianic revolt by which they might seize the throne from Caesar and the princes he had set up over the different provinces.

It seemed to be the crowning hour of success, but to Jesus Himself, it was an hour of sad and bitter shame. This was all that His year's work had come to! This was the idea they had of Him! They wanted to determine the course of His future action instead of humbly asking what He wanted to do! He accepted it as the decisive indication of the effect of His work in Galilee. He saw how shallow its results were. Galilee had judged itself unworthy of being the center from which His kingdom might extend itself to the rest of the land. He fled from their worldly desires, and the very next day, meeting them again at Capernaum, He told them how much they had been mistaken in Him. They were looking for a physical king who would give them idleness and plenty, mountains of loaves, rivers of milk, and every comfort without labor. What Jesus had to give was the bread of eternal life (John 6:35).

His teaching was like a stream of cold water directed upon the fiery enthusiasm of the crowd. From that hour, His cause in Galilee was doomed: *Many of His disciples went back and walked no more with Him* (John 6:66). It was what He intended. It was He who struck the fatal blow at His popularity. He resolved to devote Himself from then on to the few who really understood Him and were capable of being the supporters of a spiritual undertaking.

The Changed Aspect of His Ministry

Although the people of Galilee in general had shown themselves unworthy of Him, there was a considerable remnant that proved true. At the center of it were the apostles, but there were also others, probably numbering several hundred. These now became the objects of His special care. He had saved them as brands plucked from the burning (Zechariah 3:2), when Galilee as a whole deserted Him.

It must have been a time of crucial trial for the apostles. Their views were to a large extent those of the general public. They also expected a Messiah of worldly splendor. They had indeed learned to include deeper and more spiritual elements in their concept, but along with these, it still contained the traditional and earthly ones. It must have been a painful mystery to them that Jesus would so long delay the assumption of the crown.

John the Baptist's death must have been a terrible shock to the disciples. If Jesus was the Mighty One, how could He allow His friend to come to such an end? Still, they held on to Him. They showed what it was that kept them by their answer to Him, when, after the dispersion that followed the discourse at Capernaum, He asked them the sad question, *Will ye also go away?* They replied, *Lord, to whom shall we go? Thou hast the words of eternal life* (John 6:67-68). Their opinions were not clear. They were in a haze of confusion, but they knew that from Him they were getting eternal life. This held them close to Him and made them willing to wait until He would make things clear.

During the last six months He spent in Galilee, He abandoned much of His previous work of preaching and working miracles, and He devoted Himself to the instruction of these followers. He made long journeys with them to the most distant parts of the province, avoiding publicity as much as possible. We find Him at Tyre and Sidon, far to the northwest; at Caesarea Philippi, on the far northeast; and in Decapolis, to the south and east of the lake. These journeys, or flights, were due partly to the bitter opposition of the Pharisees and partly to fear of Herod, but were mainly due to the desire to be alone with His disciples.

The precious result of the journeys was seen in an incident that happened at Caesarea Philippi. Jesus asked His disciples what the popular views about Himself were, and they told Him the various theories that were flying about – that He was a prophet, that He was Elijah, that He was John the Baptist, and so on. *But whom say ye that l am?* He asked. Peter answered for them all: *Thou art the Christ, the Son of the living God* (Matthew 16:13-16). This was the deliberate and decisive conviction by which they were determined to abide, whatever might come. Jesus received the confession with great joy, and at once recognized the nucleus of the future church, the church that was to be built on the truth to which they had given expression, in those who had made it.

This realization only prepared them for a new trial of faith. From that time, we are told, Jesus began to inform them of His approaching suffering and death (Matthew 16:21). This now stood out clearly in His own mind as the only issue of His career to be looked for. He had hinted as much to them before, but with that delicate and loving consideration that always adapted His teaching to their capacity, He did not refer to it often.

Now, however, they were in some degree able to bear it, and as it was inevitable and near at hand, He kept insisting on it constantly. They themselves say that they did not in the least understand Him (Luke 18:34). In common with all their countrymen, they expected a Messiah who would sit on the throne of David and whose reign would never end. They believed that Jesus was this Messiah, and they could not understand at all that instead of reigning, He would be killed upon His arrival in Jerusalem.

They listened to Him and discussed His words among themselves, but they regarded the apparent meaning of the words as a wild impossibility. They thought He was only using one of the parables of which He was so fond, His real meaning being that the present lowly form of His work was to die and disappear, and His cause rise, as it were, out of the grave in a glorious and triumphant manner. He attempted to make things clear for them, going more and more specifically into the details of His approaching suffering, but their minds could not accept the truth.

How completely even the best of them failed to do so is shown by the frequent disagreements among them at this period as to which of them would be the greatest in the approaching kingdom (Mark 9:33-34), and also by the request of Salome for her sons that they would sit the one on the right and the other on the left hand in His kingdom (Matthew 20:20-24). When they left Galilee and went up toward Jerusalem, it was with the conviction that *the kingdom of God should immediately appear* (Luke 19:11). That is, they thought that Jesus, on arriving in the capital, would throw off the guise of humiliation He had worn up until then, and overcoming all opposition by some show of His concealed glory, would take His place on the throne of His fathers.

What were the thoughts and feelings of Jesus Himself during this year? It was a year of severe trial for Him. Now for the first time, the deep lines of care and pain could be seen upon His face. During the twelve months of successful work in Galilee, He was supported with the joy of sustained achievement, but now He became, in the truest sense, the *Man of Sorrows* (Isaiah 53:3).

His rejection by Galilee was behind Him. The sorrow that

He felt at seeing the ground on which He had bestowed so much labor turning out barren is to be measured only by the greatness of His love to the souls He sought to save, along with the depth of His obedience and devotion to the work.

In front of Him was His rejection at Jerusalem. That was now certain. It rose up and stood out constantly and unmistakably, meeting His eyes as often as He turned them to the future. It absorbed His thoughts. It was a dreadful expectation, and now that it was near, it sometimes shook His soul with a conflict of feelings that we hardly dare to even try to imagine.

Jesus was very much in prayer. This had been His delight and strength all along. In His busiest period, when He was often so tired with the labors of the day that at the approach of evening, when He was ready to fling Himself down in utter fatigue, He would nevertheless escape away from the crowds and His disciples to the mountaintop and spend the whole night in solitary communion with His Father. He never took any important step without such a night. Now, though, He was alone far more often than ever before, setting forth His case to His God with strong crying and tears.

His prayers received a wonderful answer in the transfiguration (Matthew 17:1-9). That glorious scene took place in the middle of the year of opposition, just before He left Galilee and set forth on the journey of doom. It was intended partly for the sake of the three disciples who accompanied Him to the mountaintop in order to strengthen their faith and prepare them to strengthen their brethren, but it was intended primarily for Himself. It was a great gift from His Father, an acknowledgment of His faithfulness up to this point and a preparation for what lay before Him. He conversed with His great predecessors, Moses and Elijah, who could thoroughly relate to Him and whose work His death was to fulfil, about the death He was to accomplish at Jerusalem.

Immediately after this event, Jesus left Galilee and went

south. He spent six months on His way to Jerusalem. It was part of His mission to preach the message of the kingdom over the whole land, and He did so. He sent seventy of His disciples on before Him to prepare the villages and towns to receive Him (Luke 10:1-17). In this new field, the same demonstrations that Galilee had witnessed during the first months of His labors there showed themselves: the multitudes following Him, the wonderful cures, and so forth.

We do not have adequate records of this period of His life to enable us to follow Him step by step. We find Him on the borders of Samaria, in Perea, on the banks of the Jordan River, in Bethany, and in the village of Ephraim, but Jerusalem was His goal. His face was set like a flint toward it (Isaiah 50:7). Sometimes He was so absorbed in the anticipation of what was to happen to Him there that His disciples, following His swift, silent figure along the highway, were amazed and afraid.

Now and then, indeed, He would relax for a little while, as when He was blessing the little children or visiting the home of His friends at Bethany, but His mood at this time was more stern, absorbed, and highly strung than ever before. His contests with His enemies were sharper, and the conditions that He imposed on those who offered to be His disciples were more stringent. Everything indicated that the end was drawing near. Jesus was in the grip of His grand purpose of atoning for the sins of the world, and His soul was distressed until it would be accomplished (Luke 12:50).

The catastrophe drew near quickly. Jesus made two brief visits to Jerusalem during His last six months before the final visit. On both occasions, the opposition of the authorities assumed the most menacing form. They tried to arrest Him on the first occasion (John 7:32), and they took up stones to stone Him on the second (John 8:59; 10:31). They had already issued a decree that anyone acknowledging Jesus to be the Messiah should be excommunicated (John 9:22).

However, it was the excitement produced in the popular mind by the raising of Lazarus at the very gates of the ecclesiastical citadel that finally convinced the authorities that they could not be content with anything less than His death, and they agreed on this in council (John 11:46-54). This took place only a month or two before the end came, and for a time it drove Jesus from the neighborhood of Jerusalem, but He left only until the hour came that His Father had appointed for Him.

Chapter 7

The End

The third year of His ministry approached its close, and the revolving seasons brought the great annual feast of the Passover. It is said that as many as two or three million strangers were gathered in Jerusalem on such an occasion. They not only flocked from every part of Israel to celebrate the event in which their national history began, but they came over sea and land from all the countries in which the seed of Abraham were dispersed.

They were brought together by very diverse motives. Some came with the solemn thoughts and deep religious joy of minds responsive to the memories of the venerable occasion. Some mainly looked forward to reunion with relatives and friends who had been long parted from them by living in distant places. Not a few of the lower sort brought with them the desire to profit, and were primarily intent on achieving in such a large group some important business success.

This year, though, the minds of tens of thousands were full of an unusual excitement, and they traveled to the capital expecting to see something more remarkable than they had ever witnessed there before. They hoped to see Jesus at the feast, and they entertained many unclear ideas as to what might happen in connection with Him. His name was the word that was passed from mouth to mouth most often among the groups of pilgrims that crowded along the highways, and also among the Jewish groups that talked together on the decks of the ships coming from Asia Minor and Egypt.

Undoubtedly, nearly all His own disciples were there, ardently cherishing the hope that at last in this assembly of the nation He would throw off the cloak of humility that concealed His glory, and would demonstrate His messiahship in some undeniable way. There must have been thousands from the southern portions of the country, where He had recently been spending His time, who began to have the same enthusiastic views about Him that were entertained in Galilee at the end of His first year there. Undoubtedly, multitudes of the Galileans themselves were favorably disposed toward Him and were ready to take the deepest interest in any new development of His affairs.

Tens of thousands from more distant parts, who had heard of Him but had never seen Him, arrived in the capital in the hope that He might be there and that they might enjoy the opportunity of seeing a miracle or listening to the words of the new prophet. The authorities in Jerusalem, too, awaited His coming with very mixed feelings. They hoped that some turn of events might give them the chance of at last silencing Him, but they could not help fearing that He might appear at the head of a provincial following that would place them at His mercy.

The Final Breach with the Nation

Six days before Passover began, Jesus arrived in Bethany, the village of His friends Martha, Mary, and Lazarus, which was about thirty minutes from the city on the other side of the summit of the Mount of Olives. It was a convenient place to lodge during the feast, so He stayed with His friends.

The ceremonies were to begin on a Thursday, so He arrived

there on the previous Friday. He had been accompanied the last twenty miles of His journey by an immense multitude of the pilgrims to whom He was the center of interest. They had seen Him healing blind Bartimaeus at Jericho (Mark 10:46-52), and the miracle had produced extraordinary excitement among them. When they reached Bethany, the village was ringing with the news of the recent resurrection of Lazarus, and they carried on the news to the crowds who had already arrived in Jerusalem that Jesus had come.

After resting over the Sabbath in Bethany, Jesus left on Sunday morning to proceed to the city. He found the streets of the village and the neighboring roads thronged with a vast crowd that consisted partly of those who had accompanied Him on the previous Friday, partly of other people who were traveling from Jericho and had heard of the miracles as they came along, and partly of those who, having heard that He was at hand, had flocked out from Jerusalem to see Him.

They welcomed Him with enthusiasm, and they began to shout *Hosanna to the Son of David! Blessed is He that cometh in the name of the Lord! Hosanna in the highest!* (Matthew 21:9). It was a messianic demonstration such as He had previously avoided, but now He yielded to it. He was probably satisfied with the sincerity of the allegiance paid to Him, and the hour had come when no considerations could allow Him any longer to conceal from the nation the character in which He presented Himself and the claim He made on its faith.

However, in yielding to the desires of the multitude that He should assume the style of a king, He made it unmistakable in what sense He accepted the honor. He sent for a donkey, His disciples spread their garments on it, and He rode at the head of the crowd (Matthew 21:1-11). He did not enter Jerusalem armed to the teeth or riding a warhorse, but He came as the king of simplicity and peace.

The procession swept over the brow of the Mount of Olives

and continued down the mountainside. They crossed the Kidron Valley, and mounting the slope that led to the gate of the city, passed on through the streets to the temple. The crowd swelled as they went, great numbers hurrying from all over to join it. The shouts grew louder and louder. The people broke off twigs from the palms and olives as they passed, waving them in triumph. The citizens of Jerusalem ran to their doors and leaned over their balconies to look, asking, *Who is this?* The people in the procession replied with provincial pride, *This is Jesus, the prophet of Nazareth* (Matthew 21:10-11).

It was, in fact, an entirely provincial demonstration. The citizens of Jerusalem took no part in it, but remained coldly distant. The authorities knew only too well what it meant, and they beheld it with rage and dread. They went to Jesus and ordered Him to rebuke His followers and command them to be silent, undoubtedly hinting that if He did not do so, the Roman garrison, which was stationed in the immediate vicinity, would pounce on Him and them and would punish the city for an act of treason to Caesar (Luke 19:39-40).

There is no point in the life of Jesus at which we are more motivated to ask the following questions: What would have happened if His claim had been acknowledged – if the citizens of Jerusalem had been carried away with the enthusiasm of the others, and if the animosity of the priests and scribes had given way before the torrent of public approval? Would Jesus have put Himself at the head of the nation and inaugurated an era of the world's history totally different from that which followed? No, He would not have. Jesus knew He was here for one purpose, and nothing could detract Him from the Father's will (Romans 5:19).

Jesus had formally offered Himself to the capital and to the authorities of the nation, but He was met with no response. The provincial recognition of His claims was insufficient to carry a national assent. He accepted the decision as final. The multitude expected a signal from Him, and in their excited mood would have obeyed it, whatever it might have been. He gave them none, though, and after looking around for a little while in the temple, He left them and returned to Bethany (Mark 11:11).

Doubtless, the multitude was very disappointed, and an opportunity was offered to the authorities that they did not fail to make use of. The Pharisees did not need any motivation, but even the Sadducees, those cold and arrogant friends of order, detected danger to the public peace in the state of the popular mind, and they joined themselves with their bitter enemies in their determination to suppress Him.

On Monday and Tuesday, He appeared again in the city and engaged in His old work of healing and teaching, but on the second day, the authorities interfered. Pharisees, Sadducees, Herodians, high priests, priests, and scribes were united in a common cause for once. They went to Jesus as He taught in the temple and demanded Him to tell them by what authority He did what He did (Matthew 21:23). In all the display of official attire, of social pride, and of popular renown, they set themselves against the simple Galilean while the multitudes looked on.

They entered into a sharp and prolonged dispute with Him on points selected beforehand, putting forward their champions of debate to try to entangle Him in His talk. Their specific goal was either to discredit Him with the people or to bring out something from His lips in the heat of argument that might form a reason to accuse Him before the civil authority.

So, for example, they asked Him if it was lawful to give tribute to Caesar (Mark 12:13-17). If He answered Yes, they knew that His popularity would perish in an instant, for it would be a complete contradiction of the popular messianic ideas. If, on the contrary, He answered No, they would accuse Him of treason before the Roman governor. Jesus was far more than a match for them, though.

Hour by hour He steadfastly met the attack. His

straightforwardness put their duplicity to shame. His skill in argument turned every spear that they directed at Him around to their own hearts. At last, He carried the war into their own territory and declared them guilty of such ignorance or lack of honesty that completely put them to shame before the onlookers.

Then, after He had silenced them, He let loose the storm of His indignation, delivering against them the condemnatory verbal tirade that is recorded in the twenty-third chapter of Matthew. Giving unrestrained utterance to the pent-up criticism of a lifetime, He exposed their hypocritical practices in sentences that fell like strokes of lightning and made them a scorn and a laughingstock, not only to the hearers then, but to all the world since.

It was the final break between Him and them. They had been completely humiliated before the whole people over whom they were set in authority and honor. They felt it to be intolerable, and they resolved not to lose an hour in seeking their revenge. That very evening, the Sanhedrin met in an enraged mood to devise a plan to do away with Him. Nicodemus and Joseph of Arimathea may have raised a solitary protest against their hurried proceedings, but they were indignantly silenced. The united enemies of Jesus were unanimously of the opinion that He should immediately be put to death.

Circumstances hindered their cruel haste. The forms of justice would at least have to be gone through, and besides, Jesus evidently enjoyed an immense popularity among the strangers who filled the city. What might the idle crowd do if He were arrested before their eyes? It was necessary to wait until the large group of pilgrims had left the city (Matthew 26:3-5). They had just arrived at this conclusion with great reluctance when they received a most unexpected and gratifying surprise. One of Jesus' own disciples appeared and offered to betray Him for a price.

Judas Iscariot is a byword of the human race. In his *Vision of Hell,* Dante Alighieri placed him in the lowest of the circles of the damned as the sole sharer with Satan himself of the very uttermost punishment, and the poet's verdict is that of mankind. Yet Judas Iscariot was not such a monster of iniquity as to be utterly beyond comprehension or even sympathy.

The history of his disgraceful and appalling offense is perfectly understandable. He had joined the discipleship of Jesus, as the other apostles did, in the hope of taking part in a political revolution and occupying a distinguished place in an earthly kingdom. It is inconceivable that Jesus would have made him an apostle if there had not been a need for a traitor in the midst of the disciples (Matthew 18:7; John 6:70).

That Judas Iscariot was a man of superior energy and administrative ability can be inferred from the fact that he was made the treasurer of the apostolic group. However, there was corruption, the love of money, at the root of his character that gradually absorbed all that was excellent in him and took over his life. He fed it by the petty theft that he practiced on the small sums that Jesus received from His friends for the necessities of His company and for distribution among the poor with whom He was daily mingling. He hoped to give it unrestrained gratification when He was put in charge of the finances in the new kingdom.

The views of the other apostles were perhaps as worldly to begin with as his, but the history of their interaction with their Master was totally different. They became ever more spiritual, while Judas Iscariot became increasingly worldly. The entire time that Jesus was with them, they never understood the idea of a spiritual kingdom apart from an earthly one, but the spiritual aspects that their Master had taught them to add to their physical idea grew more and more prominent until the earthly heart was eaten out of it and just the empty shell was left, to be in due time crushed and blown away. Judas' earthly views, though, became more and more consuming, and were more and more removed from every spiritual aspect. He grew impatient for their realization. Preaching and healing seemed to be a waste of time to him. The purity and unworldliness of Jesus irritated him. Why did He not bring on the kingdom at once, and then preach as much as He chose afterward?

In time, he began to suspect that there was to be no physical kingdom that he had hoped for. He felt that he had been deceived, and he began not only to despise his Master, but even to hate Him. The failure of Jesus to take advantage of the disposition of the people on Palm Sunday finally convinced him that it was useless to hold on to the cause any longer. He saw that the ship was sinking, and he was determined to get out of it.

Judas Iscariot carried out his resolution in such a way that would gratify his love of money as well as secure the favor of the authorities. His offer came to them just at the right moment. They accepted it greedily, and having arranged the price with the miserable man, they sent him away to find a convenient opportunity for the betrayal (Matthew 26:14-16). He found it sooner than they expected.

Jesus in the Prospect of Death

Christianity has no more precious possession than the memory of Jesus during the week when He stood face to face with death. Unspeakably great as He always was, it can be reverently said that He was never so great as during those days of the direst calamity. All that was greatest and tenderest, the most human and the most divine aspects of His character, were brought out as they had never been before.

Jesus entered Jerusalem well aware that He was about to die. For a whole year, that fact had been staring Him in the face constantly, and that which had been long looked for had come at last. He knew it was His Father's will, and when the hour arrived, He directed His steps with divine courage to the fatal spot (Luke 9:51). It was not, however, without a terrible conflict of feelings. The ebb and flow of the most diverse emotions – anguish and ecstasy, the most prolonged and crushing depression, the most triumphant joy and the most majestic peace – swayed back and forth within Him like the moods of a vast ocean.

Some have been unwilling to attribute to Jesus anything of that hesitation toward death that is natural to man, but that is surely without good reason. It is an instinct perfectly innocent. The very fact that He was pure and perfect may have made it stronger in Him than it is in us.

Remember how young Jesus was. He was only thirty-three. The currents of life were powerful in Him. He was full of the instincts of action. To have these strong currents rolled back and the light and warmth of life quenched in the cold waters of death must have been utterly repugnant to Him.

An incident that took place on the Monday caused Him a great shock of this instinctive pain. Some Greeks who had come to the feast expressed through two of the apostles their desire to meet with Him (John 12:20-22). There were many heathens in different parts of the Greek-speaking world who at this period had found refuge from the atheism and disgusting immorality of the times in the religion of the Jews who had settled in their midst, and they had accordingly become followers of the worship of Jehovah. These inquirers belonged to this group of people.

Their request to meet with Him shook Him with thoughts that they little dreamed of. Only two or three times in the course of His ministry does He seem to have been brought into contact with representatives of the world lying outside the limits of His own people, for His mission was exclusively to the lost sheep of the house of Israel (Matthew 15:24). On each of these occasions, though, He was met with a faith, a courtesy, and a nobility that He Himself contrasted with the unbelief, rudeness, and pettiness of the Jews. How could He help desiring to pass beyond the narrow bounds of Israel and visit nations of such simple and generous disposition?

He might often have seen visions of a career like that later achieved by Paul, who carried the glad tidings from land to land and evangelized Athens, Rome, and the other great centers of the West. What joy such a career would have been to Jesus, who felt within Himself the energy and overflowing compassion that would have been exactly appropriate! However, death was at hand to extinguish it all.

The visit of the Greeks naturally would have caused a great wave of such thoughts to come over Him. Instead of responding to their request, He might have become lost in thought, His face gloomy, and His frame shaken with the tremor of an inward conflict. He also would soon have recovered Himself, giving expression to the thoughts on which in those days He was steadying His soul: *Except a corn of wheat fall into the ground and die, it abideth alone; but if it die, it bringeth forth much fruit* (John 12:24), and *I, if I be lifted up from the earth, will draw all men unto Me* (John 12:32).

Jesus could see beyond death, as terrible and absorbing as the prospect of it was, and assure Himself that the effect of His self-sacrifice would be infinitely grander and more extensive than that of a personal mission to the heathen world could ever have been. Besides, death was what His Father had appointed for Him. This was the last and deepest consolation with which He soothed His humble and trustful soul on this as on every similar occasion: *Now is my soul troubled; and what shall I say? Father, save me from this hour: but for this cause came I unto this hour. Father, glorify Thy name* (John 12:27-28).

Death approached Him with every terrible accompaniment. He was to fall victim to the treachery of one of His own followers whom He had chosen and loved. His life was to be taken by the hands of His own nation, in the city of His heart. He had come to exalt His nation to heaven, and had loved her with a devotion nourished by the most intelligent and sympathetic acquaintance with her past history and with the great men who had loved her before Him, as well as by the sense of all that He Himself was able to do for her, but His death would bring down the affliction of a thousand curses on Israel and Jerusalem.

He showed how clearly He foresaw what was coming by His memorable prophetic discourse in the twenty-fourth chapter of Matthew, which He spoke on Tuesday afternoon to His disciples while sitting on the side of the Mount of Olives with the doomed city at His feet. He demonstrated how bitter the anguish was that it caused Him when on Sunday, even in His hour of triumph as the joyful multitude conveyed Him down the mountain road, He stopped at the point where the city burst upon the view and predicted its fate with tears and lamentations (Luke 13:34-35). It should have been the fine city's bridal day, when she should have been married to the Son of God, but the paleness of death was on her face. He who would have taken her to His heart, as the hen gathers her chickens under her wings, saw the eagles already in the air flying fast to tear her in pieces.

During the evenings of this week, He went out to Bethany. In all probability, though, He spent most of the nights alone in the open air. He wandered about in the solitude of the hilltop and among the olive groves and gardens with which the sides of the mount were covered. Many times He likely walked down the same road along which the procession had passed, and as He looked across the valley from the point where He had stopped before, at the city sleeping in the moonlight, startled the night with cries more bitter than the lamentation that rattled the multitude, repeating to His lonely heart the great truths He had uttered in the presence of the Greeks.

He was terribly alone. The whole world was against Him. Jerusalem thirsted for His life with passionate hate. The tens of thousands from the provinces turned from Him in disappointment. Not even His apostles, not even John, was in the least aware of the real situation or was able to be the confidant of His thoughts. This was one of the bitterest drops in His cup. He felt, as no other person has ever felt, the necessity of living on in the world after death. The cause He had inaugurated must not die. It was for the whole world, and it had to endure through all generations and visit every part of the globe.

After His departure, though, it would be left in the hands of His apostles, who were now showing themselves so very weak, unsympathetic, and ignorant. Were they ready for the task? Had not one of them turned out to be a traitor? Would not the cause, after He was gone (so the Tempter might have whispered), fall apart, and all His far-reaching plans for the regeneration of the world vanish like the feeble substance of a dream?

Yet He was not alone. Among the deep shadows of the gardens and upon the summits of the Mount of Olives, He sought the unfailing resource of other and less troubled days, and He still found it in His dire need. His Father was with Him, and pouring out *supplications with strong crying and tears*, He *was heard in that He feared* (Hebrews 5:7). He calmed His spirit with the sense that His Father's perfect love and wisdom were appointing all that was happening to Him and that He was glorifying His Father and fulfilling the work given to Him to do. This could banish every fear and fill Him with a *joy unspeakable and full of glory* (1 Peter 1:8).

At last, the end drew very near. The Thursday evening arrived when the Passover was eaten in every house in Jerusalem. Jesus also sat down to eat it with the Twelve. He knew that it was His last night on earth and that this was His farewell meeting with His own disciples. Happily, a full account of it has been preserved to us with which every Christian mind is familiar (Matthew 26:20-30; Mark 14:17-25; Luke 22:14-23; John 13).

It was the greatest evening of His life. His soul overflowed in indescribable tenderness and dignity. Some shadows indeed fell across His spirit in the earlier hours of the evening, but they soon passed. Throughout the scenes of the washing of the disciples' feet, the eating of the Passover, the institution of the Lord's Supper, the farewell address, and the great high-priestly prayer, the whole glory of His character shone brightly. He completely gave Himself up to the gracious impulses of friendship, His love to His own flowing forth without limit.

Then, as if He had forgotten all their imperfections, He rejoiced in the anticipation of their future successes and the triumph of His cause. Not a shadow intercepted His view of the face of His Father or dimmed the satisfaction with which He looked on His own work that was just about to be completed. It was as if the Passion was already past and the glory of His exaltation was already breaking around Him.

The reaction came very soon. Rising from the table at midnight, they passed through the streets and out of the town by the eastern gate of the city. Crossing the Kidron Valley, they reached a place at the foot of the Mount of Olives, the garden of Gethsemane, where He liked to spend time. This is where the awful and memorable events began. It was the final access of the mood of depression that had been struggling all week with the mood of joy and trust whose culmination had been reached at the supper table. It was the final onset of temptation, from which His life had never been free. However, we fear to analyze the details of the scene. We know that any thoughts of ours must be utterly unable to exhaust its meaning. How, above all, can we estimate in the slightest degree the main aspect of it – the crushing, scorching pressure of the sin of the world for which He was then atoning?

The struggle ended in a complete victory. While the poor disciples were sleeping away the hours of preparation for the crisis that was at hand, Jesus had thoroughly equipped Himself for it. He had fought down the last remnants of temptation. The bitterness of death was past, and He was able to go through the events that followed with a calmness that nothing could ruffle, and with a majesty that converted His trial and crucifixion into the pride and glory of humanity.

The Trial

Jesus had just overcome in this struggle when, through the branches of the olive trees, He saw a group of His enemies moving in the moonlight down the opposite slope, coming to arrest Him. The traitor was at their head. He was well acquainted with where his Master spent His time, and He probably hoped to find Him there asleep. For this reason, he had chosen the midnight hour for his dark deed.

It satisfied his employers well, too, for they were afraid to lay hands on Jesus in the daytime, fearing the anger of the Galilean strangers who filled the city. However, they knew how it would demoralize His friends if, conducting His trial during the night, they could present Him in the morning, after the people awoke, already a condemned criminal in the hands of the executors of the law.

They had brought lanterns and torches with them, thinking they might find their victim crouching in some cave, or supposing that they might have to pursue Him through the woods. But He came forth to meet them at the entrance to the garden, and they trembled like cowards before His majestic looks and devastating words. He freely surrendered Himself into their hands, and they led Him back to the city. It was probably about midnight. The remaining hours of the night and the early hours of the morning were occupied with the legal proceedings that had to be gone through before they could gratify their thirst for His life (Matthew 26:47-56).

There were two trials, an ecclesiastical one and a civil one, in each of which there were three stages. The first trial took place first before Annas, then before Caiaphas and an informal committee of the Sanhedrin, and lastly before a regular meeting of this court. The second took place first before Pilate, then before Herod, and lastly before Pilate again.

The reason for this double legal process was the political situation of the country. Judea, as has already been explained, was directly subject to the Roman Empire. It formed a part of the province of Syria and was governed by a Roman officer who resided at Caesarea. It was not the practice of Rome to strip those countries that she had subdued of all the forms of native government. Though she ruled with an iron hand, collected her taxes with severity, swiftly suppressed every sign of rebellion, and asserted her preeminent authority on great occasions, yet she conceded to the conquered as many symbols as possible of their ancient power.

Rome was especially tolerant in matters of religion. Thus, the Sanhedrin, the supreme ecclesiastical court of the Jews, was still permitted to try all religious causes. If the sentence passed was a capital one, though, its execution could not take place without the case being tried over again before the governor. So when a prisoner was convicted by the Jewish ecclesiastical tribunal of a capital crime, he had to be sent down to Caesarea and prosecuted before the civil court unless the governor happened to be in Jerusalem at the time. The crime of which Jesus was accused was one that naturally came before the ecclesiastical court. This court passed a death sentence on Him, but it did not have the power to carry it out. It had to hand Him on to the tribunal of the governor, who at the time happened to be in the capital, which he generally visited during the Passover.

Jesus was taken first to the palace of Annas (John 18:13). Annas was an old man of seventy who had been high priest many years earlier. He still retained the title, as did also five of his sons who had succeeded him, though his son-in-law Caiaphas was the actual high priest. His age, ability, and family influence gave him immense social weight, and he was the virtual, though not formal, head of the Sanhedrin. He did not try Jesus, but just wanted to see Him and ask a few questions. Jesus was then very soon led away from the palace of Annas to that of Caiaphas, which probably formed part of the same group of official buildings (John 18:24).

Caiaphas, as the ruling high priest, was president of the Sanhedrin, before which Jesus was tried. A legal meeting of this court could not be held before sunrise, so it must have been about six o'clock. Many of its members were already on the spot, for they had been drawn together by their interest in the case. They were eager to get to work, both to gratify their own dislike for Him and also to prevent the interference of the general public with their proceedings.

Accordingly, they resolved to hold an informal meeting at once, at which the accusation, evidence, and so forth might be made ready so that when the legal hour for opening their doors arrived, there would be nothing to do but to repeat the necessary formalities and carry Him off to the governor. This was done, and while Jerusalem slept, these eager judges hurried forward their dark designs.

They did not begin, as might have been expected, with a clear statement of the crime with which He was charged. Indeed, it would have been difficult for them to do so, for they were divided among themselves. Many things in His life that the Pharisees regarded as criminal were treated by the Sadducees with indifference. Other acts of His, like the cleansing of the temple, had enraged the Sadducees, but had pleased the Pharisees.

The high priest began by questioning Jesus as to His disciples and doctrine, evidently with the view of learning whether He had taught any revolutionary beliefs that could lead to a reason to accuse Him before the governor. Jesus repelled the insinuation, indignantly asserting that He had always spoken openly before the world, and He demanded a statement and proof of any evil He had done. This unusual reply induced one of the officials of the court to strike Jesus on the mouth with His fist – an act that the court apparently did not rebuke. That showed what amount of justice He could expect at the hands of His judges (John 18:19-23).

An attempt was then made to bring proof against Him. A number of witnesses repeated various statements they had heard Him make, out of which it was hoped an accusation might be constructed – but it turned out to be a total failure. The witnesses could not agree among themselves, and when two were finally able to unite in a distorted report of a saying of His early ministry, which appeared to have some color of criminality, it turned out to be something so insignificant that it would have been absurd to present it to the governor as the basis of a serious charge.

They were resolved on His death, but the prey seemed to be slipping out of their hands. Jesus looked on in absolute silence while contradictory testimonies of the witnesses demolished each other. He quietly took His natural position far above His judges, and they felt it. At last the president, in a moment of rage and irritation, commanded Him to speak. Why was he so loud and harsh? The humiliating spectacle going on in the witness stand and the silent dignity of Jesus were beginning to trouble even these consciences that had assembled in the dead of night.

The case had completely broken down when Caiaphas rose from his seat and, with theatrical solemnity, said: *I adjure Thee by the living God, that Thou tell us whether Thou be the Christ, the Son of God* (Matthew 26:63). It was a statement given simply to try to get Jesus to incriminate Himself. Yet He who had kept silence when He could have spoken now spoke when He could have been silent. With great solemnity He answered in the affirmative, that He was the Messiah and the Son of God. Nothing more was needed by His judges. They unanimously pronounced Him guilty of blasphemy and worthy of death.

The whole trial had been conducted with improper haste and total disregard of the formalities proper to a court of law. Everything was dictated by the desire to arrive at guilt, not justice. The same people were both prosecutors and judges. No witnesses for the defense were considered. Although the judges were undoubtedly perfectly conscientious in their sentence, it was the decision of minds long ago shut against the truth and possessed with the most bitter and revengeful passions.

The trial was now looked upon as past, the legal proceedings after sunrise being a mere formality that would only require a few minutes. Accordingly, Jesus was given up as a condemned man to the cruelty of the jailors and the mob. Then a scene ensued over which one would gladly draw a veil. There broke forth on Him a brutality of abuse that makes the blood run cold. Apparently, the members of the Sanhedrin themselves took part in it. This Man who had baffled them, impaired their authority, and exposed their hypocrisy was very hateful to them. Sadducean coldness could boil up into strong heat when it was really aroused. Pharisaic fanaticism was inventive in its cruelty. They smote Him with their fists, they spat on Him, they blindfolded Him, and in derision of His prophetic claims, they told Him to prophesy who struck Him as they took their turn hitting Him – but we will not dwell on a scene so disgraceful to human nature (Matthew 27:27-31; Luke 22:63-65).

It was probably between six and seven in the morning when they took Jesus, bound with chains, to the residence of the governor. What a spectacle that was! The priests, teachers, and judges of the Jewish nation were leading their Messiah to ask the gentiles to put Him to death! It was the hour of the nation's suicide. This was all that had come of God's choosing them, bearing them on eagles' wings (Exodus 19:4), and carrying them all the days of old, sending them His prophets and deliverers (Jeremiah 7:25-26), redeeming them from Egypt and Babylon, and causing His glory to pass before their eyes for so many centuries! Surely it was the very mockery of Providence, yet God was not mocked. His plans march down through history with resistless advancement, not waiting on the will of man. Even at this tragic hour, when the Jewish nation was turning His proceedings into ridicule, He was destined to demonstrate the depths of His wisdom and love.

The man before whose judgment seat Jesus was about to appear was Pontius Pilate, who had been governor of Judea for six years. He was a typical Roman, not of the ancient, simple breed, but of the imperial period. He was a man who had some remains of the ancient Roman justice in his soul, yet was pleasure loving, overbearing, and corrupt. He hated the Jews whom he ruled, and in times of irritation, freely shed their blood. They gratefully returned his hatred, accusing him of every crime, corruption, cruelty, and robbery. He visited Jerusalem as seldom as possible, for to someone accustomed to the pleasures of Rome with its theaters, baths, games, and pleasure-loving society, Jerusalem, with its religiousness and ever-simmering revolt, was a dreary residence. When he did visit it, he stayed in the magnificent palace of Herod the Great, as it was usual for the officers sent by Rome into conquered countries to occupy the palaces of the displaced sovereigns.

The members of the Sanhedrin and the crowd that had joined the procession as it moved on through the streets led Jesus up the broad route that led through a fine park laid out with walks, ponds, and trees of various kinds. Jesus was taken to the front of the building. The court was held in the open air, on a mosaic pavement in front of that part of the palace that united its two colossal wings.

The Jewish authorities had hoped that Pilate would accept their decision as his own and would pass the sentence they desired without going into the merits of the case. This was frequently done by provincial governors, especially in matters of religion, which, as foreigners, they could not be expected to understand. Therefore, when Pilate asked what the crime of Jesus was, they replied, *If He were not a malefactor, we would not have delivered Him up unto thee* (John 18:30).

However, Pilate was not in the mood of concession, and he told them that if he was not to try the criminal, they must be content with such a punishment as their own law permitted them to inflict. He seems to have known something of Jesus. *He knew that for envy they had delivered Him* (Matthew 27:18). The triumphal procession of Sunday was sure to have been reported to him, and the neglect of Jesus to make use of that demonstration for any political purpose might have convinced Pilate that Jesus was politically harmless. His wife's dream implied that Jesus had been the subject of conversation in the palace (Matthew 27:19), and it might have been that the polite man of the world and his lady had felt the boredom of their visit to Jerusalem relieved by the story of the young peasant enthusiast who was boldly opposing the fanatical priests.

Forced against their desire to bring forward formal charges, the Jewish authorities poured out a volley of accusations, out of which these three clearly emerged: (1) He had misled the nation, (2) He forbade people to pay the Roman tax, and (3) He set Himself up as a king (Luke 23:1-2). They had condemned Him for blasphemy in the Sanhedrin, but such an accusation would have been dealt with by Pilate, as they well knew, in the same way as it was later treated by the Roman governor Gallio when used against Paul by the Jews of Corinth (Acts 18:14-16).

Therefore, they had to invent new charges that might depict Jesus as dangerous to the government. It is mortifying to think that in doing so they resorted not only to obvious hypocrisy, but even to deliberate falsehood, for how else can we characterize the second accusation when we remember the answer He gave to their question on the same subject on the previous Tuesday (Luke 20:22-25)?

Pilate understood their pretended zeal for the Roman

authority. He knew the value of this angry concern that Rome's tax should be paid. Rising from his seat to escape the fanatical cries of the mob, Pilate took Jesus inside the palace to examine Him. It was a solemn moment for him, although he did not know it.

What a terrible fate it was that brought Pilate to this spot at this time! There were hundreds of Roman officials scattered throughout the empire who were conducting their lives on the same principles as his was guided by. Why did it fall to him to bring them to bear on this case? He had no idea of the issues he was deciding. The criminal may have seemed to him a little more interesting and perplexing than others, but Jesus was only one of hundreds who were constantly passing through his hands. It could not have occurred to him that even though he appeared to be the judge, both he and the system he represented were on their trial before One whose perfection judged and exposed every man and every system that approached Him.

Pilate questioned Jesus in regard to the accusations brought against Him, asking especially if He pretended to be a king. Jesus replied that He made no such claim in the political sense, but only in a spiritual sense, as King of the Truth (John 18:37-38). This reply would have grabbed the attention of any of the nobler spirits of heathendom who spent their lives in the search for truth, and it might have been stated in such a way as to find out whether there was any response in Pilate's mind to such a suggestion. However, he had no such desire, and he dismissed it with a laugh. He was convinced, though, as he had supposed, that there was nothing of the instigator or messianic revolutionist behind this pure, peaceful, and melancholy face. So, returning to the tribunal, Pilate announced to Jesus' accusers that he had acquitted Him.

The announcement was received with shouts of disappointed rage and the loud reiteration of the charges against Him. It was a thoroughly Jewish spectacle. This fanatical mob had overcome the wishes and decisions of their foreign masters many times by the sheer force of outcry and obstinacy. Pilate should have immediately released and protected Jesus, but he was a true son of the system in which he had been brought up – the political art of compromise and maneuver.

Amid the cries with which they assailed his ears, he was glad to hear one that offered him an excuse to get rid of the whole business. They were shouting that Jesus had stirred up the people *throughout all Jewry, beginning from Galilee unto this place* (Luke 23:5). It occurred to Pilate that Herod, the ruler of Galilee, was in town, and that he could get rid of this troublesome matter by handing it over to Herod, for it was a common practice in Roman law to transfer an accused criminal from the tribunal of the territory in which he was arrested to that of the territory in which he lived. Therefore, Pilate sent Jesus away in the hands of his bodyguard, and accompanied by His unwavering accusers, to the palace of Herod.

They found this ruler, who had come to Jerusalem to attend the feast, in the midst of his small-minded court of flatterers and festive companions, and surrounded by the bodyguard that he maintained in imitation of his foreign masters. He was delighted to see Jesus, whose fame had so long been ringing through the territory over which he ruled.

Herod had only one thought in life: his own pleasure and amusement. He came up to the Passover merely for the sake of the excitement. The appearance of Jesus seemed to promise a new sensation, of which he and his court were often greatly in need, for he hoped to see Jesus work a miracle (Luke 23:8). Herod was a man utterly incapable of taking a serious view of anything, and he even overlooked the business about which the Jews were so eager, for he began to pour out a flood of rambling questions and remarks without pausing for any reply.

At last, however, he exhausted himself and waited for the response of Jesus, but he waited in vain, for Jesus did not give him one word of any kind (Luke 23:9). Herod had forgotten the murder of John the Baptist, every impression being written as if on water in his characterless mind; but Jesus had not forgotten it. He felt that Herod should have been ashamed to look John the Baptist's friend in the face. He would not stoop to even speak to a man who could treat Him as a mere wonder-worker, who might purchase His judge's favor by exhibiting His skill.

Jesus looked with sad shame on the one who had abused himself until there was no conscience or manliness left in him, but Herod was utterly incapable of feeling the annihilating force of such silent disdain. He and his men of war did not consider Jesus worthy of respect and consideration. They threw a white robe over His shoulders in imitation of that worn at Rome by candidates who were seeking support for political office to indicate that He was a candidate for the Jewish throne, but it was one so ridiculous that it would be useless to treat Jesus with anything but contempt. Herod sent Jesus back to Pilate in this way, and in this way Jesus retraced His weary steps to the Roman court of justice (Luke 23:11).

A course of procedure then ensued on the part of Pilate by which he became an image of the opportunist that would be displayed to the centuries in the light falling on him from Christ. It was evidently his duty, when Jesus returned from Herod, to immediately pronounce the sentence of acquittal. But instead of doing so, he resorted to what he thought would be more advantageous to him, and being hurried on from one false step to another, was finally hurled down the slope of complete betrayal to principle. He proposed to the Jews that since both he and Herod had found Him innocent, he should scourge and then release Him (Luke 23:13-17). The scourging would be a gesture to appease their rage, and releasing Jesus would be a tribute to justice.

The carrying out of this outrageous proposal was, however, interrupted by an incident that seemed to offer Pilate one more way of escape from his difficulty. It was the custom of the Roman governor on the Passover morning to release to the people any single prisoner they might desire. It was a privilege highly prized by the people of Jerusalem, for there were always plenty of prisoners in jail who, by rebellion against the detested foreign bondage, had made themselves the heroes of the multitude.

At this stage of Jesus' trial, the mob of the city, pouring out from street and alley in an agitated manner, came streaming up the avenue to the front of the palace, shouting for this annual gift. The shouts of the crowd were for once welcome to Pilate, for he saw in them a loophole of escape from his disagreeable position. It turned out, however, to be a noose through which he was slipping his neck.

Pilate offered the life of Jesus to the mob. They hesitated for a moment, but they had a favorite of their own. They wanted to free Barabbas, a noted leader of revolt against the Roman domination. Voices instantly began to whisper busily in their ears, putting every art of persuasion into motion in order to induce the people not to accept Jesus. The members of the Sanhedrin, despite the zeal they had manifested the hour before for law and order, did not hesitate to take the side of the champion of insurrection. The whispering voices succeeded only too well in poisoning the minds of the people, who began to shout for their own hero, Barabbas.

What, then, shall I do with Jesus? asked Pilate. He expected them to answer, "Give us Him too," but he was mistaken. The authorities had done their work successfully. The cry came from ten thousand throats: *Let Him be crucified!* (Matthew 27:22). Like priests, like people. It was the acceptance by the nation of the decision of its leaders.

Pilate, completely baffled, angrily asked, *Why, what evil hath He done?* (Matthew 27:23). But he had put the decision into their hands. They were now thoroughly fanaticized, and they yelled out, *"Away with Him; crucify Him, crucify Him!"* (Luke 23:18-21).

Pilate did not yet mean to sacrifice justice completely. He still had a move in reserve, but in the meantime, he sent Jesus away to be scourged – the usual preliminary to crucifixion. The soldiers took Him to a room in their barracks, and they feasted their cruel instincts on His sufferings. We will not describe the shame and pain of this revolting punishment. What must it have been to Him, with His honor and love for human nature, to be handled by those rough and rude men and to look so closely at human nature's utmost brutality!

The soldiers enjoyed their work and heaped insult upon cruelty. When the scourging was over, they set Jesus down on a seat, found an old rejected cloak, and flung it on His shoulders in derisive imitation of the royal purple. They thrust a reed into His hands for a scepter. They stripped some thorn twigs from a nearby bush, twisted them into the rough resemblance of a crown, and crushed down their piercing spikes upon His brow. Then, passing in front of Him, each of them in turn bent their knee, while at the same time spitting in His face. Then, plucking the reed from His hand, they smote Him with it over the head and face (Matthew 27:27-31; Mark 15:15-20).

At last, having satisfied their cruelty, they led Him back to the court wearing the crown of thorns and the purple robe. The crowds raised shouts of mad laughter at the soldiers' joke. Pilate thrust Jesus forward so that everyone could see Him, and then he cried out, *Behold the man!* (John 19:5). He meant that surely there was no use doing any more to Him. He was not worth their effort. Could one so broken and wretched do any harm? How little he understood his own words!

That *Behold the man!* is heard all over the world and draws the eyes of all generations to that marred countenance. Behold! As we look, the shame is gone. It has lifted off Jesus and has fallen on Pilate himself, on the soldiers, on the priests, and on the angry crowd. His bright glory has scorched away every speck of disgrace and covered the crown of thorns with a hundred points of flaming brightness.

Pilate understood the spirit of the people he ruled just as poorly when he supposed that the sight of the misery and helplessness of Jesus would satisfy their thirst for vengeance. Their objection to Him all along had been that one so poor and unambitious would claim to be their Messiah, and the sight of Him now, scourged and scorned by the Roman soldiers, yet still claiming to be their King, raised their hate to madness so that they cried louder than ever, *Crucify Him, crucify Him* (John 19:6).

Now at last, they angrily expressed the real charge against Him, which had been burning at the bottom of their hearts all along, and which they could no longer suppress: *We have a law,* they cried, *and by that law He ought to die, because He made Himself the Son of God* (John 19:7).

These words struck a chord in Pilate's mind that the people had not thought of. In the ancient traditions of his native land, there were many legends of sons of the gods who in the days of old had walked the earth in humble appearance so that they were indistinguishable from common men. It was dangerous to meet them, for an injury done to them might bring down on the offender the wrath of the gods, their fathers. Faith in these ancient myths had long died out because no men were seen on earth who were so different from their neighbors as to require such an explanation.

But in Jesus, Pilate had discerned an inexplicable something that affected him with an uncertain terror. Now the words of the mob, *He made Himself the Son of God* (John 19:7), came like a flash of lightning. They brought back out of the recesses of his memory the old, forgotten stories of his childhood. The words revived the heathen terror that formed the theme of some of the greatest Greek dramas – that of unknowingly committing a crime that might evoke the dire vengeance of heaven. *Might not Jesus be the Son of the Hebrew Jehovah*, so his heathen mind reasoned, *just as Castor and Pollux were the sons of Jupiter?*

Pilate quickly took Jesus inside the palace again, and looking at Him with new awe and curiosity, asked Him where He was from (John 19:9). Jesus did not answer him one word. Pilate had not listened to Him when He might have explained everything to him. Pilate had wronged his own sense of justice by scourging Him, and if a man turns his back on Christ when He speaks, the hour will come when he will ask and receive no answer.

The proud governor was both surprised and irritated. He demanded, *Speakest Thou not to me? Knowest Thou not that I have power to crucify Thee, and have power to release Thee?* (John 19:10). Jesus responded with the indescribable dignity of which the brutal shame of His torture had in no way robbed Him: *Thou couldst have no power at all against Me, except it were given thee from above* (John 9:11).

Pilate had boasted of his power to do what he chose with the prisoner, but in reality he was very weak. He came forth from his private interview determined at once to release Him. The Jews saw it in his face, and it made them bring out their last weapon that they had been keeping in reserve the whole time: they threatened to complain against him to the emperor. This was the meaning of the cry with which they interrupted his first words: *If thou let this man go, thou art not Caesar's friend* (John 19:12). This had been in the minds of the people and in the mind of Pilate all throughout the trial. It was this that made him so determined. There was nothing a Roman governor dreaded so much as a complaint against him sent by his subjects to the emperor.

It was especially dangerous at this time, for the royal throne was occupied by a gruesome and suspicious tyrant who delighted in disgracing his own servants. He would erupt in a moment at the whisper of any of his inferiors favoring anyone else for the royal power. Pilate knew only too well that his administration could not hold up to inspection, for it had been cruel and corrupt in the extreme. Nothing is so certain to keep someone from doing the good that he wants to do as the evil of his past life. This was the blast of temptation that finally swept Pilate off his feet – just when he had made up his mind to obey his conscience. He was not a hero who would obey his convictions at any cost. He was a complete man of the world, and he saw at once that he must surrender Jesus to their will.

However, Pilate was not only full of rage at being so completely repulsed, but he was also full of an overpowering religious dread. Calling for water, he washed his hands in the presence of the multitude, and cried, *I am innocent of the blood of this just Person* (Matthew 27:24). Pilate washed his hands when he should have made use of them. Blood is not very easily washed off. The mob, now completely triumphant, scorned his misgivings, filling the air with the cry, *His blood be on us and on our children!* (Matthew 27:25).

Pilate felt the insult sharply, and turning on them in his anger, determined that he, too, would have his triumph. Thrusting Jesus forward more prominently into view, he began to mock them by pretending to regard Him as really their king, and asking, *Shall I crucify your king?* It was now their turn to feel the sting of mockery, and they cried out, *We have no king but Caesar* (John 19:15). What a confession from Jewish lips! It was the surrender of the freedom and the history of the nation. Pilate took them at their word, and immediately handed Jesus over to be crucified.

The Crucifixion

The people had succeeded in taking their victim out of Pilate's unwilling hands, *and they took Jesus and led Him away* (John 19:16). In time, they were able to gratify their hatred to the uttermost, and they hurried Him off to the place of execution with every demonstration of inhuman triumph. The actual executioners were the soldiers of the governor's guard, but in moral significance the deed belonged entirely to the Jewish authorities. They could not leave it in charge of those who were given the task of carrying out the punishment, but with undignified eagerness they led the procession themselves in order to feast their vindictiveness on the sight of His sufferings.

By this time it must have been about ten o'clock in the morning. The crowd at the palace had been gradually increasing. As the fatal procession, headed by the members of the Sanhedrin, passed on through the streets, it attracted great multitudes. It happened to be a Passover holiday, so there were thousands of people who were waiting for any excitement. All those especially who had been injected with the fanaticism of the authorities poured forth to witness the execution. It was, therefore, through the midst of a multitude of cruel and unsympathetic onlookers that Jesus went to His death.

The spot where He suffered cannot now be identified. It was outside the gates of the city, and was undoubtedly the common place of execution. It is usually called Mount Calvary, but there is nothing in the Gospels to justify such a name,[5] nor does there seem to be any hill in the neighborhood on which it could have taken place. The name Golgotha, *place of a skull* (Matthew 27:33; Mark 15:22; John 19:17), might signify a skull-like cliff, but more probably refers to the dreadful relics of the tragedies happening there that might have been lying around. It was probably a wide, open space in which a multitude of spectators could assemble. It appears to have been on the side of a much-traveled path, for in addition to the spectators who were gathered around, there were others walking by who joined in mocking the Sufferer.

Crucifixion was an unspeakably horrible death. As Cicero, who was well acquainted with it, says, it was the most cruel and shameful of all punishments. "Let it never," he adds, "come near the body of a Roman citizen; nay, not even near his thoughts,

---

5   See Luke 23:33. "Calvary" is mentioned in some Bible versions, such as the King James Version. It is from a Latin word, *calvaria*, which means "skull," as in "the place of the skull."

or eyes, or ears." It was reserved for slaves and revolutionaries whose end was meant to be marked with special infamy. Nothing could be more unnatural and revolting than to suspend a living man in such a position.

The idea of crucifixion seems to have been suggested by the practice of nailing up vermin in a kind of revengeful amusement on some exposed place. If the end had come with the first strokes in the wounds, it would still have been a terrible death, but the victim usually lingered two or three days – with the burning pain of the nails in his hands and feet, the torture of burdened veins, and worst of all, his intolerable thirst, all constantly increasing. It was impossible to keep from moving the body so as to try to get relief from each new aspect of pain, yet every movement brought new and excruciating agony.

We gladly turn away from the gruesome sight now to think how Jesus triumphed over the shame, the cruelty, and the horror of it by His strength of soul, His submission to His Father's will, and His love. We consider how, just as the sunset with its crimson glory makes even the rancid pool of water blaze like a shield of gold and how it drenches with brilliance the most contemptible object held up against its beams, Jesus converted the symbol of slavery and wickedness into a symbol for whatever is most pure and glorious in the world.

The head hung free in crucifixion so that Jesus was able not only to see what was going on beneath Him, but also to speak. He uttered seven sentences at intervals that have been preserved to us. They are seven windows by which we can still look into His very mind and heart and learn the impressions made on Him by what was happening. They show that He retained intact the peace of mind and majesty that had characterized Him throughout His trial and demonstrated in their fullest exercise all the qualities that had already made His character illustrious.

He triumphed over His sufferings not by the cold severity of a Stoic, but by selfless love. When He was fainting beneath the

burden of the cross in the Via Dolorosa, He forgot His fatigue
in His concern for the daughters of Jerusalem and their children
(Luke 23:28). When they were nailing Him to the cross, He was
absorbed in a prayer for His murderers. He quenched the pain
of the first hours of crucifixion by His interest in the penitent
thief (Luke 23:39-43) and His care to provide a new home for
His mother (John 19:26-27). He never was more completely
Himself – the absolutely unselfish Worker for others.

It was, indeed, only through His love that He could be deeply
wounded. His physical sufferings, though intense and prolonged,
were not greater than those that have been endured by many
other sufferers, unless the virtue of His being may have height-
ened them to a degree that is inconceivable to other people. He
did not linger more than five hours – a space of time so much
briefer than usual that the soldiers who were about to break His
legs were surprised to find Him already dead (John 19:32-33).

His worst sufferings were those of the mind. He whose very
life was love, who thirsted for love as the deer longs for the water
brooks (Psalm 42:1), was encircled with a sea of hatred and of
dark, bitter, infernal rage that surged around Him and flung
its waves up around His cross. His soul was spotlessly pure.
Holiness was its very life, but sin pressed itself against it, try-
ing to force upon it its loathsome touch that His soul wanted
desperately to avoid.

The members of the Sanhedrin, or the council, took the
lead in venting on Him every possible expression of contempt
and malicious hate, and the populace faithfully followed their
example (John 11:47-54). These were the men He had loved and
still loved with an unquenchable affection, and they insulted,
crushed, and trampled on His love. Through their lips, the Evil
One reiterated again and again the temptation by which, all His
life, He had been assaulted – to save Himself and win the faith
of the nation by some display of supernatural power made for
His own advantage. That angry mass of human beings, whose

faces, distorted with fury, glared upon Him, was a perfect example of the wickedness of the human race. His eyes had to look down on it, seeing its callousness, its sadness, and its dishonor of God. Its exhibition of the shame of human nature was like a group of spears converged in His chest.

There was a still more mysterious anguish. Not only did the world's sin press itself on His loving and holy soul in those near Him, but it also came from afar – from the past, the distant, and the future – and converged on Him. He was bearing the sin of the world, and the consuming fire of God's nature, which is the reverse side of the light of His holiness and love, flamed forth against Him to scorch it away. So it pleased the Lord to *put Him to grief* (Isaiah 53:10) when He who knew no sin was made sin for us (2 Corinthians 5:21).

These were the sufferings that made the cross dreadful. After about two hours, Jesus withdrew Himself completely from the outer world and turned His face toward the eternal world. At the same time, a strange darkness spread across the land (Matthew 27:45). Jerusalem trembled beneath a cloud whose murky shadows looked like a gathering doom. Golgotha was essentially deserted. Jesus hung on the cross for a long while, silent amid the darkness without and the darkness within, until at last, out of the depths of an anguish that human thought will never fathom, there issued the cry, *My God, my God, why hast Thou forsaken Me?* (Psalm 22:1; Matthew 27:46). It was the moment when the soul of the Sufferer touched the very bottom of His misery.

However, the darkness passed from the landscape and the sun shone forth again. The spirit of Christ, too, emerged from its eclipse. With the strength of victory won in the final struggle, He cried, *It is finished!* (John 19:30). Then, with perfect serenity, He breathed out His life on a verse of a favorite psalm: *Father, into Thy hands I commend My spirit* (Luke 23:46, quoting Psalm 31:5).

The Resurrection and Ascension

There was never an enterprise in the world that seemed more completely at an end than did that of Jesus on the last Old Testament Sabbath. Christianity died with Christ and was laid with Him in the sepulcher. It is true that when we look back and see the stone rolled to the mouth of the tomb, we experience little emotion, for we are in the secret of Providence and know what is going to happen. But when Jesus was buried, there was not a single human being who believed He would ever rise again before the day of the world's doom.

The Jewish authorities were thoroughly satisfied of this. Death ends all controversies, and it had settled the one between Him and them, triumphantly in their favor. He had put Himself forward as their Messiah, but had hardly any of the marks that they looked for in one with such claims. He had never received any important national recognition. His followers were few and uninfluential. His career had been short. He was in the grave. Nothing more was to be thought of Him.

The breakdown of the disciples had been complete. When He was arrested, *they all forsook Him and fled* (Mark 14:50). It is true that Peter had followed Him to the high priest's palace, but only to fall more disgracefully than the rest. John followed Him even to Golgotha, and may have hoped against hope that at the very last moment He would descend from the cross to ascend the messianic throne. But even the last moment went by and nothing happened. What remained for them except to return to their homes and their fishing as disappointed men who would be ridiculed for the rest of their lives for foolishly following a pretender, and who would be asked where the thrones were on which He had promised to seat them?

Jesus had, indeed, foretold His sufferings, death, and resurrection, but the disciples never understood these sayings. They forgot them or gave them an allegorical turn, and when

He was actually dead, these sayings did not provide them with any comfort whatsoever. The women came to the sepulcher on the first Christian Sabbath, not to see it empty, but to embalm His body for its long sleep (Mark 16:1). Mary ran to tell the disciples, not that He was risen, but that the body had been taken away and laid she knew not where (John 20:2). When the women told the other disciples how He had met them, *their words seemed to them as idle tales, and they believed them not* (Luke 24:11). Peter and John, as John himself informs us, *knew not the Scripture, that He should rise from the dead* (John 20:9). Could anything be more heartbreaking than the words of the two travelers to Emmaus: *We trusted that it had been He which should have redeemed Israel* (Luke 24:21)? When the disciples met together, *they mourned and wept* (Mark 16:10). There were never people more utterly disappointed and dispirited.

Now, though, we can be glad that they were so sad. They doubted so that we could believe. For how is it to be explained that a few days later these very people were full of confidence and joy, their faith in Jesus had revived, and the enterprise of Christianity was again in motion with a far greater vitality than it had ever before possessed?

They say that the reason for this was that Jesus had risen, and they had seen Him. They tell us about their visits to the empty tomb and how He appeared to Mary Magdalene, to the other women, to Peter, to the two on the way to Emmaus, to ten of them at once, to eleven of them at once, to James, to the five hundred, and so forth (e.g., 1 Corinthians 15:3-8). Are these stories credible? They might not be if they stood alone, but the alleged resurrection of Christ was accompanied by the indisputable resurrection of Christianity. How is the latter to be accounted for except by the former?

It might rightly be said that Jesus had filled their minds with royal dreams that He failed to realize. It could be said that once they had caught sight of such a magnificent career, they were unable to return to their fishing nets, and so invented this story in order to carry on the scheme on their own account. It could be said that they only imagined that they saw what they tell about the Risen One.

However, the remarkable thing is that when they resumed their faith in Him, they were found to be no longer pursuing worldly goals, but intensely spiritual ones. They were no longer expecting thrones, but persecution and death – yet they addressed themselves to their new work with a breadth of intelligence, an intensity of devotion, and a faith in results that they had never shown before.

As Christ rose from the dead in a transfigured body, so did Christianity. It had put off its carnality. What brought about this change? They say it was the resurrection and the sight of the risen Christ, but their testimony is not the proof that He rose. The incontestable proof is the change itself – the fact that they had suddenly become courageous, hopeful, believing, and wise. They suddenly had noble and reasonable views of the world's future and were equipped with sufficient resources to establish the church, convert the world, and build Christianity in its purity among men.

Between the last Old Testament Sabbath and a few weeks later when this astonishing change had undeniably taken place, some event must have happened that can be regarded as a sufficient cause for such a great effect. Only the resurrection answers the difficulties of the problem, and is therefore proved by a demonstration far more effective than any testimony could possibly be. It is a good thing that this event is capable of such a proof, for if Christ is not risen, then our faith is useless (1 Corinthians 15:14, 17). However, if He is risen, then all of His miraculous life becomes credible, for this was the greatest of all the miracles. His divine mission is demonstrated, for it must have been God who raised Him up, and the most assuring glance that history offers is given into the realities of the eternal world.

The risen Christ lingered on earth long enough to fully satisfy His adherents of the truth of His resurrection. They were not easily convinced. The apostles treated the reports of the holy women with scornful disbelief. Thomas doubted the testimony of the other apostles. Some of the five hundred to whom Jesus appeared on a Galilean mountain doubted their own eyesight, and they only believed when they heard His voice. The loving patience with which He treated these doubters showed that, although His bodily appearance was somewhat changed, He was still the same in heart as ever. This was movingly shown, too, by the places that He visited in His glorified form. They were the old meeting places where He had prayed and preached, labored and suffered: the Galilean mountain, the well-beloved lake, the Mount of Olives, the village of Bethany, and above all, Jerusalem, the fateful city that had murdered her own Son, but which He could not cease to love.

There were obvious indications, though, that He no longer belonged to this lower world. There was a new reserve about His risen humanity. He forbade Mary to touch Him when she would have kissed His feet (John 20:17). He appeared in the midst of His own disciples with mysterious suddenness, and just as suddenly vanished out of their sight (Luke 24:31, 36; John 20:19). He was with them now only occasionally, no longer allowing them the constant and familiar communion of former days. Then, at the end of forty days, when the purpose for which He had remained on earth was fully accomplished and the apostles were ready in the power of their new joy to carry the message of His life and work to all nations, His glorified humanity was received up into that world to which it rightfully belonged (Mark 16:19; Luke 24:51; Acts 1:9).

Conclusion

No life ends, even for this world, when the body in which it has been made visible for a little while disappears from the face of the earth. It enters into the stream of the ever-swelling life of mankind, and it continues to act there with its whole force forevermore. Indeed, the true magnitude of a human being can often only be measured by what this afterlife shows him to have been.

So it was with Christ. The modest narrative of the Gospels scarcely prepares us for the outburst of creative force that issued from His life when it appeared to have ended. His influence on the modern world is the evidence of how great He was, for there must have been as much in the cause as there is in the effect. It has blanketed the life of man and caused it to blossom with the vigor of a spiritual spring. It has absorbed into itself all other influences, just as a mighty river flowing along the center of a continent receives tributaries from a hundred hills. Its quality has been even more exceptional than its quantity.

The most important evidence of what He was, though, is to be found neither in the general history of modern civilization nor in the public history of the visible church, but in the experiences of the succession of genuine believers who, with linked hands, stretch back to touch Him through the Christian generations. The experience of innumerable souls, redeemed by Him from themselves and from the world, proves that history was cut in two by the appearance of One who would breathe new life into them, who was not a mere link in the chain of common men, but was One whom the race could not from its own resources have produced. He was the perfect Type, the Man of men.

The experience of innumerable consciences, the most sensitive to both their own sinfulness and the holiness of the Divine Being that the world has ever seen, yet who were able to rejoice in a peace with God that has been found to be the most powerful result of a holy life, proves that in the midst of the ages an act of reconciliation was worked out by which sinful people can be made one with a holy God.

The experience of innumerable minds, rendered blessed by the vision of a God who, to the eye that has been purified by the Word of Christ, is so completely Light that in Him there is no darkness at all (1 John 1:5), proves that the final revelation of the Eternal to the world has been made by One who knew Him so well that He could not Himself have been less than Divine.

The life of Christ in history cannot cease. His influence increases more and more. The unreached nations are waiting until it reaches them. All great discoveries of the modern world, every development of ideas that are more just, that are of greater virtue, and that are more excellent in mankind are only new ways to help us know and understand Him more.

Hints for Teachers and Questions for Students

It will be observed that what has been attempted in the preceding pages has been to lift the main details of our Lord's life into prominence and to clearly point out its decisive events, keeping the details as brief as possible. These details are more popularly known than any other part of human knowledge. What most readers of the Gospels need is a concise summary that will naturally arrange itself so that the life of Jesus can be seen as a whole, and an attempt has here been made to supply this need.

However, in a Bible class course that extends beyond twelve or fifteen lessons, more details might be beneficial. Therefore, a more detailed outline is included here, along with a few questions on the text intended to encourage students to further thought and inquiry.[6]

As tools for the teacher, I would recommend:

- Samuel James Andrews' *The Bible Student's Life of Our Lord*, an unpretentious but excellent book, in which the apologetic difficulties in the details of the life are treated with much candor and success

- Augustus Neander's *Life of Jesus Christ*, the best life, in my opinion, that has been published, although sadly marred by too great concessions to the spirit of denial, which had reached its climax in Germany at the time when it was written

- Frederic Farrar's *The Life of Christ*, John Cunningham Geikie's *The Life and Words of Christ*, or Alfred Edersheim's *The Life and Times of Jesus the Messiah*, which will lend vividness to the teacher's remarks.

- These books, along with a good commentary on the Gospels, a harmony of the Gospels, and a handbook of Bible geography, are sufficient.

- Happy will the teacher be who has, in addition to the above books, James Hastings' *Dictionary of Christ and the Gospels* or his *Dictionary of the Bible*.

---

6   For another good source to take a closer look at the miracles and parables of Jesus, see the three-volumes of Charles Spurgeon's *Life in Christ*, updated by and available from Aneko Press. Also beneficial will be J. C. Ryle's *Expository Thoughts* on the different gospels, also available from Aneko Press.

Preliminary Characteristics of the Four Gospels

Matthew

- Hebrew thought and diction.

- Well acquainted with Old Testament in the original.

- Frequent quotations, *That it might be fulfilled* (Matthew 1:22; 2:15, 23; 4:14; 8:17; 12:17; 13:35; 21:4; 27:35)

- His aim was to prove that Jesus was the Messiah.

- *The kingdom* is very prominent (Matthew 3:2; 4:17, 23; 5:3, 10, 19, 20, etc.).

- Methodical groupings and combinations, such as groups of parables (chapters 13, 24, 25) and of miracles (chapters 8 and 9).

Mark

- Graphic and epic.

- Believed to be a pupil of Peter, whose fiery spirit pervades his book.

- Poetic objectivity and minuteness.

- Details as to the looks and gestures of Jesus, the amazement He created, etc.

- His aim was to show how Jesus proved Himself to be the messianic King by a succession of astonishing deeds.

- Stormful haste. Very frequently uses terms such as "forthwith," "immediately," etc.

Luke

- More of a trained historian than the other Evangelists.

- Hellenic grace of style.

- Series of cameos.

- Gives reasons for events.

- Philosophic.

- Psychological comments.

- Pauline spirit and universality.

- Christ is not only for the Jews, but for all of mankind.

- The genealogy of Jesus is traced back beyond Abraham (Luke 3:23-38).

John

- Supplies what the other Evangelists omitted.

- Dwells especially on the work of Jesus in Judea.

- Tells of Jesus' private interviews, His interior life, and His most profound and mysterious sayings.

- Lyric fervor, wisdom, and beauty of farewell discourses.

When Were Our Gospels Written?

See Constantine von Tischendorf's little book of this name, Johann Lange's *Life of Christ, Life of Christ* by Bernhard Weiss, Brooke Westcott's *Study of the Gospels,* or Moffat's, Peake's, Bacon's, or Zahn's *Introduction to the New Testament.*

It would probably be out of place in a Bible class course to go at any length into this vexed and vast question. The most important point is the date of John's gospel. See Christopher Luthardt's *St. John: The Author of the Fourth Gospel*, Henry Watkins' *Modern Criticism Considered in Its Relation to the Fourth Gospel*, or William Sanday's *Authorship and Historical Character of the Fourth Gospel*.

The man who hides from himself what Christianity and the Christian revelation are takes the parts of it to pieces and persuades himself that he can account for all the pieces without divine interposition. Here is something from the Jews and something from the Greeks. Here are miracles that may be partly odd natural events, partly nervous impressions, and partly gradually growing legends. Here are books, of which we may say that this element was contributed by this party, and the other by that, and the general coloring by people who held partly of both. In such ways as these, Christianity is taken down and spread over several centuries. But when your operation is done, the living whole draws itself together again, looks you in the face, refuses to be conceived in that manner, reclaims its scattered members from the other centuries back to the first, and reasserts itself to be a great burst of coherent life and light, centering in Christ. In the same way, you could take apart a living tissue and say there is here only nitrogen, carbon, lime, and so forth; but the energetic peculiarities of life going on before your eyes would refute you by the palpable presence of a mystery unaccounted for. (Principal Rainy, New College Inaugural Address, 1874)

Other Sources of the Life of Jesus

References in Josephus, Tacitus, etc., are of little importance except to show how little insight these observers had into the most important event of their times. Jewish history and antiquities explain the period. Ancient history exhibits "the fullness of time."

Fresh information has recently been sought from two sources:

1. *Agrapha* are sayings of Jesus not found in the Gospels. These have been laboriously collected by Alfred Resch, whose results have been sifted by James Ropes in *Die Spruche Jesu*.

2. In John Thompson's *Books Which Influenced Our Lord and His Apostles*, a source from which much new light is expected by some, the literature produced between the Old Testament and the New Testament is discussed, which has all been collected by D. E. Kautzsch in *Die Apokryphen und Pseudepigraphen des alten Testaments*, and *Apocrypha Pseudepigrapha* by R. H. Charles.

The Annunciation

Prophecy of John the Baptist's birth. Visit of Mary to Elizabeth. Events connected with John's birth.

1. For what reasons can the life of Christ be regarded as the most interesting subject of human thought?

2. Why are the first three Evangelists called the Synoptists?

3. What is the meaning of the saying that the scenery of Israel is the fifth Gospel?

Chapter 1

There are three opinions as to the brothers and sisters of Jesus: (1) they were His full brothers and sisters, (2) they were the children of Joseph by a former marriage, and (3) they were His cousins. The Greek word for "brethren" is used with such latitude as to cover all these meanings. See the note in E. H. Plumptre's *General Epistle of James with Notes and Introduction.*

David McCalman Turpie's *Old Testament in the New* provides much interesting information on the ways in which Christ and the apostles quote the Old Testament Scriptures, showing where they adhere literally to the Hebrew text, where they adhere to the Septuagint, and where they deviate from both. A recent book on the same subject is Wilhelm Dittmar's *Vetus Testamentum in Novo.* In *Jesu Muttersprache*, Arnold Meyer has attempted to prove that Jesus habitually spoke and preached in Aramaic, and this is accepted on the Continent. But even if this were His mother tongue, it does not necessarily mean that He preached in it. The only elaborate argument on the subject in English, that of the late Dr. Roberts of St. Andrews, ends in the conclusion that He preached in Greek. Do not the fragments of Aramaic preserved in the Gospels convey the impression that He fell back on the mother tongue in moments of emotion, but that He habitually used another language?

When it is said at any point in His later life that He retired to "the mountain," it is generally needless to inquire which mountain. It was any mountain that was accessible. There were few places where there was not mountainous land around.

- To what extent must this star have been supernatural?

- What portions of Scripture were most quoted by Jesus?

- What is the Septuagint?

- What indications are there that Jesus did not generally speak on the spur of the moment, but thought His discourses carefully out beforehand?

Chapter 2

On the subjects discussed in the first half of this chapter, the first one hundred pages of Eduard Reuss' *Christian Theology in the Apostolic Age* will be found full of light.

It would be useful here to give a sketch of the history of the interval between the Old and New Testament histories, of which so little is popularly known. See John Skinner's *Historical Connection Between the Old and New Testaments,* William Fairweather's *From the Exile to the Advent,* or R. Waddy Moss' *From Malachi to Matthew.* On the various methods in which Rome ruled subject territories, see William Ramsay's *Manual of Roman Antiquities.*

To learn about the arrangements of the synagogue, see Frederic William Farrar's *Life of Christ.* The ritual of Presbyterian churches is a close imitation of that of the synagogue, whereas Catholic ritual imitates that of the temple. Also see Marcus Dods' *Presbyterianism Older than Christianity.*

On the Pharisees, see J. B. Mozley's remarkable discourse in his *University Sermons,* and compare Julius Wellhausen's treatise, *The Pharisees and the Sadducees.* Farrar's *Life of Christ* will provide useful illustration of what is said in the text in regard to the scribes. A wealth of information on these topics can be found in Adolf Hausrath's *History of New Testament Times* or in Emil Schürer's *History of the Jewish People in the Time of Jesus Christ. The Jewish Religion in the Time of Jesus* by Georg Wilhelm Hollmann might also be beneficial.

A somewhat lengthened lesson might be introduced here on the Old Testament prophecies and types. See Patrick Fairbairn's *Interpretation of Prophecy* and *Typology of Scripture.*

- Give parallels from the history of Christianity.

- Compare the aspects of society in our country at present with those of Israel in the time of Christ.

- Give the names of people who are said to have been waiting for the Messiah, and compile from the Song of Mary (Luke 1:46-55) and elsewhere an outline of what their expectations were.

- From various references in the Gospels, make an outline of the ideas that the scribes and the general public had of the Messiah and His era.

Chapter 3

John the Baptist, excellent subject for class essay. See *John the Baptist* by Henry Roberts Reynolds and *The Last of the Prophets* by J. Feather.

John Owen has a remarkable chapter on this subject in his work on the Holy Spirit.

Potuit non peccare, or *Non potuit peccare*? Was Christ able to sin, or was He not able to sin? For a discussion of this topic, see Carl Ullmann's *Sinlessness of Jesus.*

The official significance of the temptation of Jesus is explained in the text, but it would also be good to discuss its personal significance for the character of Jesus and His relation to His Father. There was temptation to unbelief, presumption, and pride. See *Studies in the Gospels* by Richard Chenevix Trench, Adolphe Monod's three sermons on *Jesus Tempted in the Wilderness* (*Jesus Tente Au Desert*), and also *The Temptation of Our Lord* by Norman Macleod.

On the plan of Jesus, see *Life of Jesus Christ in Its Historical Connection and Historical Development* by Augustus Neander.

- Give examples of people who have achieved a great life's work in a short time and died young (e.g., Robert Murray McCheyne, David Brainerd).

- It has been asserted that Jesus changed His plan

because He first addressed Himself to the Jewish nation as a whole, but afterward organized the Christian church from the nucleus of a few disciples. What would you say in answer to such a view?

- What was the difference between John's baptism and Christian baptism?

- Some think that Jesus and John had met before; is that likely?

- Compile the biblical passages that speak of the influence of the Holy Spirit on the human nature of Jesus.

- Narrate John Milton's account of the temptation in *Paradise Regained.*

- To learn about the geography of Israel, see Arthur Stanley's *Sinai and Palestine, In Connection with Their History*; George Adam Smith's *The Historical Geography of the Holy Land*; William McClure Thomson's *The Land and the Book*; Archibald Henderson's *Palestine*; and Henry Baker Tristram's *Fauna and Flora of Palestine.*

Chapter 4

There were two cleansings of the temple, the one at the beginning (John 2:13-17) and the other at the close of the ministry (Luke 19:45-46). Such double accounts of similar events in the Gospels have been seized upon as examples of the tendency in speech to multiply one event into two. However, it is forgotten that this is a tendency not only of speech, but of action, and that when a person has done anything once, there is a likelihood that he will do it again.

The Great Feasts

1. The Passover, held in April, just before the harvest began.

2. Pentecost, held fifty days after the Passover, at the conclusion of the corn harvest and before the harvesting of grapes.

3. The Feast of Tabernacles, held in autumn after all the fruits had been gathered in.

4. The Feast of Dedication, which Jesus once attended, took place in December.

Collect the sayings of John about Jesus, and of Jesus about John.

Chapter 5

On Galilee, see Frederic Farrar's *Life of Christ*. Augustus Neander's account of the methods of Jesus is very valuable. For the convenience of teachers who might want to follow out in detail the incidents of each period, the following list of the events of this year can be given (see *The Bible Student's Life of Our Lord* by Samuel James Andrews):

- Second call of Peter, Andrew, James, and John.

- Busy Sabbath: preaches in synagogue of Capernaum and cures demoniac; heals Peter's mother-in-law; cures many after sunset.

- Next morning goes to mountain to pray, then sets out on a preaching tour in the neighboring towns, in one of which He cures a leper.

- Returns to Capernaum; heals a man carried by four friends, forgiving his sins; accused of blasphemy; walks by seaside and teaches; calls Matthew; accused as Sabbath-breaker for allowing His disciples to pluck ears of corn and for healing a withered hand on the Sabbath.

- Retires to a mountain; calls the Twelve; delivers the Sermon on the Mount.

- Again in Capernaum; heals centurion's servant.

- Another preaching tour; raises widow's son at Nain; receives a message from John the Baptist and compliments him; dines with Simon the Pharisee and is anointed by the woman who was a sinner; parable of the Two Debtors.

- In Capernaum again; casts out a mute demon; visited by His mother and brothers; teaches from a boat.

- Crossing the lake, He calms a storm; cures demoniacs in country of Gadarenes.

- Back in Capernaum; Matthew's feast; raises Jairus' daughter and cures the woman with an issue of blood.

- On another tour of the Galilean towns, He revisits Nazareth; sends forth the Twelve; hears of John the Baptist's murder.

- It would be a useful exercise for the members of a class to illustrate these events with quotations from the Gospels.

Some of the many questions in reference to the possibility and the proof of miracles would naturally, in an extended course, be discussed here; see *Eight Lectures on Miracles* by James Bowling Mozley and *Divine Immanence* by John Richardson Illingworth. I do not think that there can be any reasonable doubt that our Lord gave His endorsement to the view that the demoniacs were actually possessed by evil spirits.

The acknowledgment that John the Baptist did not work any miracles is a strong point against the mythical theory. If it was natural for that age, as this theory asserts, to surround people with a halo of miracle who had impressed its imagination, why were not miracles attributed to John the Baptist? Very few are narrated even of Paul.

Connection of the work of Christ with the fate of nature.

Monographs on our Lord's miracles by Trench, Bruce, Laidlaw, and Steinmeyer.

On the teaching of Jesus, many good remarks will be found in *Great Teacher: Characteristics of Our Lord's Ministry* by John Harris. On the form of the parables, the introductory chapters in *Notes on the Parables of Our Lord* by Richard Chenevix Trench are good.

A much fuller account of what Jesus taught than is given in this book would be very desirable in an extended course, and could be gathered from the related portions of any handbooks of New Testament theology, such as those by Weiss, Beyschlag, Holtzmann, Feine, Weinel, Schlatter, and Stevens. Monographs on the subject are D. H. Meyer's *Le Christianisme du Christ,* Alexander Balmain Bruce's *Kingdom of God,* Hans Hinrich Wendt's or George Barker Stevens' *Teaching of Jesus,* and George Holley Gilbert's *The Revelation of Jesus.* Also see James Robertson's *Our Lord's Teaching* and David Morrison Ross' *The Teaching of Jesus.* There is much good literature on the parables of our Lord, such as that by Lisco, Trench, Arnot, Bruce, Dods, Taylor, Goebel, Jiilicher, Bugge, and van Koetsfeld.

See *The Kingdom of God Biblically and Historically Considered: The Tenth Series of the Cunningham Lectures* by James Stuart Candlish.

James Stalker's *Christology of Jesus: Being His Teaching Concerning Himself According to the Synoptic Gospels* supplies much information about the voluminous foreign literature on the teaching of Christ.

Christ's method of dealing with inquirers.

On the mission of the apostles, see Alexander Balmain Bruce's, *Training of the Twelve.*

Sketches of the leading apostles. The difficulty about the choice of Judas is only a fragment of the larger difficulty of reconciling the foreknowledge of God with man's free will.

For some of the remarks on the character of Jesus, I am indebted to Theodor Keim's *Geschichte Jesu.* Also compare Horace Bushnell's fine chapter on the character of Jesus in *Nature and the Supernatural,* Phillips Brooks' *Influence of Jesus,* and Francis Greenwood Peabody's *Jesus Christ and the Christian Character.*

See Carl Ullmann's *Sinlessness of Jesus.*

The two names by which Jesus called Himself – Son of man and Son of God – should be explained here. See Willibald Beyschlag's *Die Christologie des Neuen Testaments,* Vincent Henry Stanton's *The Jewish and the Christian Messiah,* or Guillaume Baldensperger's *Das Selhstbewusstsein Jesu im Lichte der Messianischen Hoffnungen Seiner Zeit,* as well as Edwin Abbott's *Son of Man: Contributions to the Study of the Thoughts of Jesus.*

- Mention as many great and good men as you can who have been called crazy or insane.

- What reasons can be suggested why Jesus sometimes used means and sometimes dispensed with them?

- What proof of the credibility of the gospel account of the miracles of Christ is provided by the confession that John worked none?

- Is it correct to speak of the miracles of Jesus as interruptions of the order of nature?

- Can the popular ideas about the wicked life of

Mary Magdalene be proved from the Gospels to be incorrect?

- With what evidence would you support the statement that Jesus, though the Man of Sorrows, was yet the most joyful of men?

- What portions of the Old Testament especially justify this description of the Eastern mind?

- Enumerate the parables of Jesus, and make a list of His other most remarkable figures of speech.

- How would you account for the great difference between the circle of Christ's ideas recorded by the Synoptists, and the circle of His ideas that we find in John?

- Which of the Evangelists uses the phrase "the kingdom of heaven," and what does it mean?

- Enumerate the private conversations of Jesus.

- What proof of their Master's supernatural greatness is given by the character and achievements of the Twelve?

- What conclusions can you draw from the fact that Jesus was sinless?

- Prove the divinity of Christ as fully as possible from the first three Evangelists, and show that it is a complete mistake to allege that it is taught only in John's gospel.

Chapter 6

The events of this year were the following:

1. Leaving Capernaum, Jesus crosses the lake; feeds five thousand; walks on the sea; rescues sinking Peter.

2. Again in Capernaum; discourse on bread of life; many disciples forsake Him; He says that Judas has a devil; discussion about eating bread with unwashed hands.

3. Long journey to Tyre and Sidon, where He cures the Syro-Phoenician woman's daughter; then to Decapolis, where He heals a deaf man and feeds four thousand; returns to Capernaum.

4. Leaves it again; cures blind man at Bethsaida; visits Caesarea Philippi; the great confession; the Transfiguration; cures demoniac boy; announces His death.

5. Again, in Capernaum; pays tribute.

6. Visit to Jerusalem at the Feast of Tabernacles; teaches in temple; attempt to arrest Him; Nicodemus seeks justice for Him; adulteress brought to Him; heals blind man, who then argues with the rulers; parable of the Good Shepherd.

7. Final departure from Galilee.

8. Journey toward Jerusalem; John and James want to rain fire on a Samaritan village; the Seventy sent out; journey through Perea; parable of the Good Samaritan; the Lord's Prayer; mute demoniac healed; encounters with Pharisees; parable of the Rich Fool; "signs of the times"; heals infirm woman; warned against Herod.

9. At the Feast of Dedication in Jerusalem; visit to Bethany; nearly stoned in the city.

10. Retires to Bethabara; while at a feast in a Pharisee's house on the Sabbath, He heals man of dropsy and tells the parable of the Great Supper; several parables were directed against the Pharisees.

11. Raising of Lazarus.

12. Retires to Ephraim; heals ten lepers; more parables against the Pharisees; blesses children; the rich young man; Salome's request; Jericho – Bartimaeus, Zacchaeus; then on to Bethany.

Luke gives by far the fullest account of the events of the period between the final departure from Galilee and the final arrival at Bethany, chapters 9-24.

It would be a good exercise for the students to gather texts from the Gospels illustrating these events.

See Robert Mackintosh's *Christ and the Jewish Law.*

The effect of John the Baptist's death on the followers of Jesus is put in a very memorable yet exaggerated way in *PhiloChristus: Memoirs of a Disciple of the Lord* by Edwin Abbott.

The Feast of Tabernacles and the Feast of Dedication.

• How far does conscientiousness justify conduct? Illustrate your answer by historical parallels to the conduct of the Pharisees.

• Can you show from the Old Testament that miracles were not necessarily evidences of a divine mission?

Chapter 7

Details of Jesus' life that were not referred to in this book: supper at Bethany and anointing of Jesus by Mary; the barren fig tree cursed; the second purging of the temple; widow's mites; several parables; details of the parting meeting with the apostles;

the miracles that accompanied His death; details of His burial; restoration of Peter.

The Passover took place this year on April 6.

The anachronism of using the days of the Christian week will be condoned for the sake of clearness.

I cannot adopt the theory of Judas' career expounded in Thomas De Quincey's well-known and brilliant essay "Judas Iscariot" – that he thought Jesus was too unworldly and hesitating and so threw Him into a position in which He would be compelled to exhibit His divine glory, but with no thought that He would allow Himself to be executed. Its strong point is the suicide of Judas, which is held to have shown a kind of nobility in his nature. But it is inconsistent, I think, with his theft and his kiss, and especially with the tone in which Scripture speaks of him.

Josephus' account of the destruction of Jerusalem might be given here.

On the difficult question whether it was the Passover supper that Jesus ate with the apostles, and whether John places the crucifixion on the same day as the other Evangelists, see Samuel James Andrews' *The Bible Student's Life of Our Lord*, Excursus X from Frederic Farrar's *Life of Christ*, and David Smith's *The Days of His Flesh: The Earthly Life of Our Lord and Savior Jesus Christ*. See also Brooke Foss Westcott's *Gospel of the Resurrection* and William Milligen's *Resurrection of Our Lord*.

The silence of Jesus.

On the legal aspects of the trial, see *The Trial of Jesus Christ* by Dr. A. Taylor Innes.

Herod was ultimately banished to Gaul.

Pilate was also ultimately deprived of his position, and is said by Eusebius to have eventually killed himself, "wearied with misfortunes." His wife, under the name of Claudia Procula, is included among the Roman Catholic saints.

The cross was probably of the form in which it is familiarly represented, although sometimes it was like the letter *T* or the letter *X*. It only raised the victim a foot or two above the ground. The soldier was able to reach the lips of Jesus with a hyssop stalk. Otto Zoeckler has an excellent monograph on the cross of Christ.

See William Paley's *Evidences of Christianity*, especially part 1.

Details of Peter's fall. It was when being taken from the committee room, where He had been informally tried, to a barrack room, where He was detained until the legal hour for opening court arrived, that *the Lord turned and looked upon Peter*. In some ways, the most important appearance of all may have been that to His own brother James. On its results and their apologetic value, see *Imago Christi* by James Stalker.

For more about the appearances of Jesus after His resurrection, see *Appearances of our Lord after the Passion* by Henry Barclay Swete, and also a work on the same subject by Friedrich Loofs.

- Quote a passage from Acts to show from how many different countries the scattered Jews gathered to the annual feasts.

- Discuss the meanings of *Hosanna* and *Hallelujah*.

- Who were the people not of Abraham's seed with whom Jesus came in contact in the course of His ministry?

- Gather the texts in which the majesty of our Lord's appearances is mentioned.

- In what points was the trial of Paul that resulted in his being sent to Rome similar to that of Jesus?

- What were the seven last sentences of Jesus?

- What is the meaning of the comment that the Christian church is the best biography of Christ?

Author Biography

James Stalker was born in Crieff, Scotland, on February 21, 1848. He was educated at the University of Edinburgh, and he was ordained as a minister of the Free Church of Scotland in 1874. He began his ministry at St. Brycedale, in Kirkcaldy, in that same year, and in 1887 he began pastoral duties at St. Matthew's in Glasgow. He was also a professor of church history at the Free Church College in Glasgow. James Stalker was a widely known preacher of his day in Scotland and America. He also authored many books, the two best known of which are his *Life of Jesus Christ* and his *Life of St. Paul.*

He was known for speaking out from the pulpit against the social sins of his day. He supported the movement for revival and supported the meetings of D. L. Moody and Ira Sankey when they came to Scotland in 1873. Rev. Stalker often visited America, where he preached at many colleges and seminaries, including at Yale in 1891. He gave some advice to the students at Yale about preaching. He said:

> It is true of every appearance that a minister makes before a congregation. Unless he has spent the week with God and received Divine communication, it would be better not to enter the pulpit or open his

mouth on Sunday at all. There ought to be on the spirit, and even on the face of a minister, as he comes forth before men, a ray of the glory that was seen on the face of Moses when he came down among the people with God's message from the mount.

James Stalker encouraged ministers to spend much time in communion with God. "The soul must be in touch with God and enjoy golden hours of fresh revelation." He explained the most common cause of failure in pastoral ministry:

Either we have never had a spiritual experience deep and thorough enough to lay bare to us the mysteries of the soul; our experience is too old, and we have repeated it so often that it has become stale to us; we have made reading a substitute for thinking; we have allowed the number and the pressure of the duties of our office to curtail our prayers and shut us out of our studies; or we have learned the professional tone in which things ought to be said, and we can fall into it without present feeling. Power for work like ours is to be acquired in secret; it is only the man who has a large, varied, and original life with God who can go on speaking about the things of God with fresh interest; but a thousand things happen to interfere with such a prayerful and meditative life. . . . The hearers may not know why their minister, with all his gifts, does not make a religious impression on them; but it is because he is not himself a spiritual power.

James Stalker preached and wrote with power, for He communed with God, faithfully followed Jesus, walked in the Spirit, and boldly proclaimed the gospel. James Stalker died on February 5, 1927.

Other Similar Titles

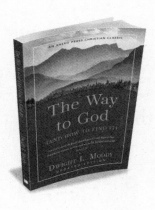

The Way to God, by Dwight L. Moody

There is life in Christ. Rich, joyous, wonderful life. It is true that the Lord disciplines those whom He loves and that we are often tempted by the world and our enemy, the devil. But if we know how to go beyond that temptation to cling to the cross of Jesus Christ and keep our eyes on our Lord, our reward both here on earth and in heaven will be 100 times better than what this world has to offer.

This book is thorough. It brings to life the love of God, examines the state of the unsaved individual's soul, and analyzes what took place on the cross for our sins. *The Way to God* takes an honest look at our need to repent and follow Jesus, and gives hope for unending, joyous eternity in heaven.

Available where books are sold.

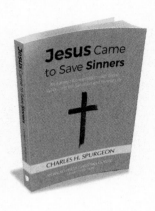

Jesus Came to Save Sinners, by Charles H. Spurgeon

This is a heart-level conversation with you, the reader. Every excuse, reason, and roadblock for not coming to Christ is examined and duly dealt with. If you think you may be too bad, or if perhaps you really are bad and you sin either openly or behind closed doors, you will discover that life in Christ is for you too. You can reject the message of salvation by faith, or you can choose to live a life of sin after professing faith in Christ, but you cannot change the truth as it is, either for yourself or for others. As such, it behooves you and your family to embrace truth, claim it for your own, and be genuinely set free for now and eternity. Come and embrace this free gift of God, and live a victorious life for Him.

Available where books are sold.

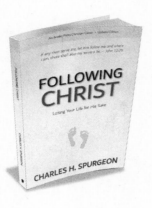

Following Christ, by Charles H. Spurgeon

You cannot have Christ if you will not serve Him. If you take Christ, you must take Him in all His qualities. You must not simply take Him as a Friend, but you must also take Him as your Master. If you are to become His disciple, you must also become His servant. God-forbid that anyone fights against that truth. It is certainly one of our greatest delights on earth to serve our Lord, and this is to be our joyful vocation even in heaven itself: *His servants shall serve Him: and they shall see His face* (Revelation 22:3-4).

Available where books are sold.

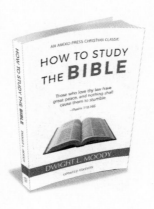

How to Study the Bible, by Dwight L. Moody

There is no situation in life for which you cannot find some word of consolation in Scripture. If you are in affliction, if you are in adversity and trial, there is a promise for you. In joy and sorrow, in health and in sickness, in poverty and in riches, in every condition of life, God has a promise stored up in His Word for you.

This classic book by Dwight L. Moody brings to light the necessity of studying the Scriptures, presents methods which help stimulate excitement for the Scriptures, and offers tools to help you comprehend the difficult passages in the Scriptures. To live a victorious Christian life, you must read and understand what God is saying to you. Moody is a master of using stories to illustrate what he is saying, and you will be both inspired and convicted to pursue truth from the pages of God's Word.

Available where books are sold.

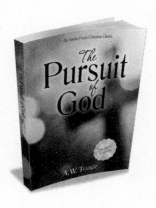

The Pursuit of God, by A. W. Tozer

To have found God and still to pursue Him is a paradox of love, scorned indeed by the too-easily-satisfied religious person, but justified in happy experience by the children of the burning heart. Saint Bernard of Clairvaux stated this holy paradox in a musical four-line poem that will be instantly understood by every worshipping soul:

> We taste Thee, O Thou Living Bread,
> And long to feast upon Thee still:
> We drink of Thee, the Fountainhead
> And thirst our souls from Thee to fill.

Come near to the holy men and women of the past and you will soon feel the heat of their desire after God. Let A. W. Tozer's pursuit of God spur you also into a genuine hunger and thirst to truly know God.

Available where books are sold.